D1710015

LATIN AMERICAN
AIR WARS
AND AIRCRAFT 1912-1969

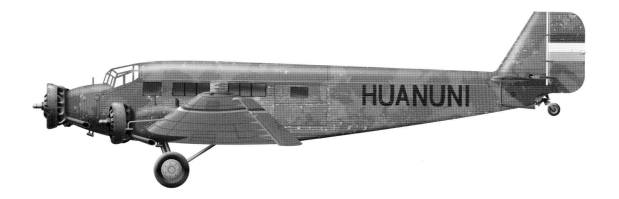

DAN HAGEDORN

Illustrated by Tim Brown

ACKNOWLEDGEMENTS

This book started life as a proposal to Hikoki Publications to document the use of the North American B-25 Mitchell medium bomber series in Latin America. As it developed, the leadership of Hikoki felt that a much broader, comprehensive history of the use of aircraft in action in Latin America was warranted.
Five years passed while the accumulated data of more than 40 years of research was massaged, edited, reviewed and molded into a coherent form.
Needless to say, the contents of this work owes an enormous debt to a very large number of aviation historians, archivists, military and air attachés, past and present, as well as photographers and artists.
Readers downloading my main narrative text will note "Special Thanks" expressed in a number of chapters to persons, without whom, the text could not have been presented.
Besides these, the following are owed a special debt. First and foremost, my life-long friends Dr. Gary Kuhn and John M. Davis, my colleagues at the National Air and Space Museum, Allan Janus, Lawrence Wilson, David Schwartz and Melissa Keiser, and the dean of aviation history in Brazil, Captain Carlos Dufriche.
I also indebted to Mario Overall and the core leadership of the Latin American Aviation Historical Society, as well as James V. Sanders of the Small Air Forces Clearing House. My thanks also to Tim Brown for the spectacular art work, Michael Bird for his endurance and fortitude, and Robert Forsyth and Eddie Creek for work on production.
Last but not least, my sincere thanks to all of the named – and unnamed – air attaché's that have reported so accurately since the very dawn of aviation in Latin America, and who, through their often blunt language, breathed life into the narrative of a by-gone era.

Dan Hagedorn

Fairfax, Virginia May 2005

First published in 2006 by

Hikoki Publications Limited
Friars Gate Farm
Mardens Hill
Crowborough
East Sussex TN6 1XH
England

Email: info@hikokiwarplanes.com
Web: www.hikokiwarplanes.com

© Dan Hagedorn

Project Editor: Robert Forsyth

Production Management: Chevron Publishing and Tim Brown

Design and layout: Tim Brown

© Colour Artwork and cover illustration: Tim Brown
Special thanks to Annette Hunt

ISBN 1 902109 44 9

All rights reserved. No part of this book may be reproduced or transmitted in any form or by any means electronic or mechanical, including photocopying, recording or by any information storage without permission from the Publisher in writing. All enquries should be directed to the Publisher.

Printed in Singapore

LATIN AMERICAN
AIR WARS
AND AIRCRAFT 1912-1969

DAN HAGEDORN

ILLUSTRATED BY TIM BROWN

HIKOKI
PUBLICATIONS

CONTENTS

How to download the accompanying text files for Latin American Air Wars

An easy-to-use Guide

Readers wishing to view and/or download Dan Hagedorn's accompanying narrative to this book should simply visit the Hikoki Publications website at www.hikokiwarplanes.com and click on either the Latin American Air Wars download icon or go to 'Our Books' and click on the Latin American Air Wars jacket icon.

By clicking on these icons, you will be taken to an easy-to-use download guide.

ABOUT THIS BOOK

This book, and the accompanying on-line text downloads, is an experiment in recording aviation history. We urge the reader to do something that most readers don't do: take a moment and read the following, so that an understanding of the organization and evolution of this work might be achieved.

When the publisher agreed that this project was an important addition to the literature of aviation history, the author had presented him and his production staff with what seemed to be an insurmountable problem. If the full text, with all supporting illustrations, captions, maps and original color drawings were published conventionally, the end product would have been a mammoth tome with a retail cost far beyond the reach of the vast majority of readers interested in the subject matter.

Normally, in the course of producing a book, compromise on the quantity of text, illustrations and associated content are reached based on the likely economic reality of the finished product. Inevitably, the author is obliged to surrender sections and images that are painfully gained, with the net result that the reader acquires a diluted version of the original work. In the course of preparing this book, the publisher and author agreed that such a compromise simply was not acceptable. The text accompanying the illustrations, which we believe you will find comprehensive and extremely detailed, needed to see the light of day. A book such as this, often referred to in the publishing world as a "fringe" title, usually has one chance. But the sheer size of the manuscript, if published conventionally, was an challenging obstacle. The introductory chapter, dealing with the multi-faceted use of aircraft throughout the length of the Mexican revolutionary period, at some 144 manuscript pages, was equal in length to many monographs on a single subject – and this was but the first of 34 following chapters! Clearly, another way had to be found.

With the advent of the personal computer, now enjoying world-wide acceptance and utilization, a means to satisfy the traditional joy of holding a hard-bound book, with new and interesting illustrations and thorough captions, matched with a comprehensive text, was found. What is more, it has enabled the publisher to market this book at a cost to the reader that is not only reasonable but, if measured in terms of the text in the accompanying on-line downloads, is actually an amazing bargain.

When visiting the publisher's website at www.hikokiwarplanes.com, the reader will find an easy-to-use guide on downloading the chapter files, the titles of which will correspond to the chapters in this book.

The author of this work produced his first nine books on a manual typewriter, and the editing and word-count issues that were part and parcel of that ancient process were daunting. This approach, a mix of digital and conventional publishing, to a conservative aero-historian in his sixth decade, seems an eminently satisfactory use of the wonderful new technology, and we sincerely hope that you will agree.

Dan Hagedorn, Fairfax, Virginia, May 2005

Publisher's note

Many readers - especially in Europe and other countries outside of the Americas - will be unfamiliar with the geography and history of Latin America. The author has therefore set the stage, as it were, at the beginning of each of the 34 chapters, with a brief explanation of the immediate causes of the conflict.

The maps in this illustrated history are based on the best available documentary sources, though these are in some cases unavoidably incomplete, and in some instances the place names are not to be found on modern maps.

The downloadable text of some 175,000 words goes into the historical and political background in very much more detail, as well as describing each military conflict - air-to-air and air-to-surface battles - much more fully and vividly than space allows in this volume. We recommend readers to avail themselves of this valuable resource at no cost. Full instructions on downloading appear opposite.

Michael Bird

Publisher

THE HISTORICAL SETTING

ABOVE: By mid-1942, Argentina's neutrality had resulted in every one of her Martin 139WAA medium bombers being grounded for parts. These aircraft constituted the Argentine Army's primary strike and coastal patrol force during the Second World War. Here, Juan Peron and his junta inspect a line-up, including by 1944 the camouflaged '505'. (via Fred Young).

For the purposes of this book and the text in the accompanying downloads, the author has arbitrarily decided upon the inclusive term "Latin America" to describe the region of the world that is documented herein.

Latin America is further defined as including all of the traditional nations in mainland South America, all of the traditional nations in Central America, and the same for the Caribbean, and I have included the great North American nation of Mexico for reasons that will become obvious.

Some assumptions need to be addressed at the outset. Europeans, North Americans and peoples of the nations of the Middle and Far-East have all benefited from and, in many instances suffered from, the advent and evolution of the airplane. The great industrial powers led the way in the design, fielding and development of, especially, military aircraft. Great feats of arms, adventure and commerce have resulted. And while this is reasonably well documented in a multitude of books and periodicals, Europe, North America and Asia have not, contrary to that literature and the exhibits mounted in numerous museums, had an exclusive on aviation. Latin Americans arguably recognized the utility of the aircraft, and engaged even some of the earliest examples, in warfare and commerce from the very dawn of aviation. Indeed, one of the very earliest uses of aircraft was during the War of the Triple Alliance involving Brazil and Paraguay between 1867-1868, when Brazil fielded a corps of military balloon observers.

With regard to the motivations that led to these events, there are a number of explanatory factors that can be offered. The very internal features of each military service involved, including often the hierarchical structure, level of professionalism, corporate interests

and, indeed, the officers' class backgrounds all played a part at one time or another. Community identities, self-image and political attitudes also entered into the equation, as did the politicization of the populace and ordinary citizens and, not least, economic factors. Through it all, however, it must be stressed that none of these human experiences are unique to Latin America, and any suggestion that the so-called "Latino temperament" was operative is ethnocentric and inappropriate. Pride and nationalism are not unique to the region. The men and, occasionally, women, involved in these events were possessed of the same human characteristics as anywhere and, as well, were shaped by the environment and stage upon which their lives unfolded.

The airmen themselves, in nearly every episode described herein, took to the air almost in spite of enormous difficulties. Latin America, until relatively recently, has been an enormously diverse mixing bowl for all phases of the aviation experience. In the first two decades, French, British, Italian and North American interests competed for what were viewed as fresh new markets, and, inevitably, they brought their own brand of training, control, tactical and disciplinary philosophy along with them. It is little wonder that it was not at all uncommon to find some Latin American air organizations with pilots who could fly only one type of aircraft, based on the training syllabus they had been weaned on.

Equipment, often bizarre and not found anywhere else on the planet, was equally challenging to buy, transport, erect, service and maintain. Although those nations with a fairly well developed education system formed the vital infrastructure necessary to accomplish these tasks, for the most part, they were carried out in the years prior to the 1940s

Cavalier-rebuilt F-51Ds and TF-51Ds were truly beautiful aircraft, seen here in Bolivian service during the late 1960s (see Chapter 33). (via Fred Young).

T-33A-1-LO FAG-721, showing details of the exotic color scheme whilst in Guatemalan service in January 1970. (via Fred Young).

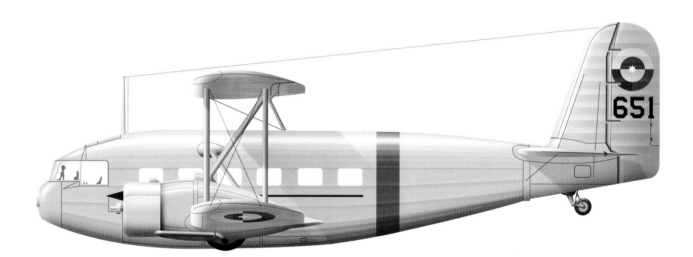

Curtiss-Wright BT-32 Condor, coded '651' Colombian Aviación Militar, Colombia, 1934

by a mere handful of gifted, sometimes completely illiterate ground crew. These men, and the pilots who often ignored their warnings, were hard-pressed to keep up with the astonishing pace of aviation advances. But some of them did not need to. An unknown number of mechanics in numerous Latin American air forces never serviced any aircraft other than the immortal North American AT-6 Texan during the course of a 30 year service career. Although accomplished, they were usually unable to transition easily to the jets that were soon passed into their care, and the learning curve was daunting.

Making use of the aircraft placed in their care by the Governments and rebel factions of the region is the grist for this mill, and the stories and events leading to placing aircraft into harms way are, seemingly, never really simple to understand.

These events are, unfortunately, often trivialized, and few of them can be found in the relatively small number of historical treatments of the region and, what is more, on the omnipotent Internet. But these things most assuredly did happen, and they are all part of the panoply of the evolution of aviation of the 20th Century, the first century of manned flight.

Dan Hagedorn
Fairfax, VA May 2005

MAPS

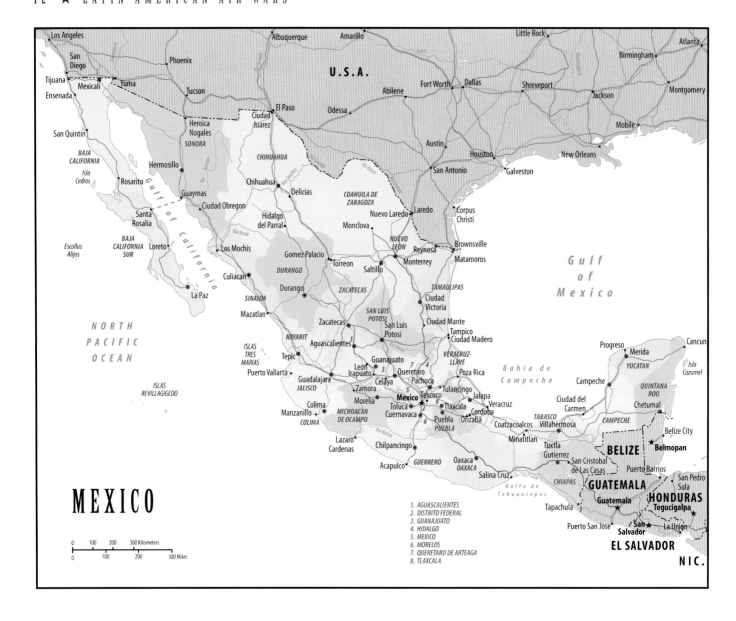

MEXICO

Los Angeles
San Diego
Tijuana
Mexicali
Ensenada
Yuma
Tucson
San Quintin

BAJA CALIFORNIA

Isla Cedros

Rosarito

Santa Rosalia

BAJA CALIFORNIA SUR

Escollus Alijos

Loreto

Gulf of California

La Paz

NORTH PACIFIC OCEAN

ISLAS TRES MARIAS

ISLAS REVILLAGIGEDO

Albuquerque
Amarillo
Little Rock
Atlanta

U.S.A.

Phoenix
Birmingham
Montgomery
Mobile

Red R.

El Paso
Ciudad Juarez
Odessa
Abilene
Fort Worth
Dallas
Shreveport
Jackson

Heroica Nogales

SONORA

CHIHUAHUA

Austin
Houston
New Orleans
Galveston

Hermosillo

Chihuahua
Delicias

COAHUILA DE ZARAGOZA

San Antonio

Rio Bravo

Guaymas
Ciudad Obregon

Hidalgo del Parral

Monclova

NUEVO LEON

Nuevo Laredo
Laredo
Corpus Christi

Los Mochis

Rio Verde

Gomez Palacio
Torreon
Saltillo
Monterrey
Reynosa
Matamoros
Brownsville

Gulf of Mexico

Culiacan

DURANGO

Durango

ZACATECAS

TAMAULIPAS

Ciudad Victoria

Mazatlan

SINALOA

Zacatecas

SAN LUIS POTOSI

San Luis Potosi

Ciudad Mante
Tampico
Ciudad Madero

NAYARIT

Aguascalientes

Rio Verde

Bahia de Campeche

Progreso
Cancun
Merida

Tepic

VERACRUZ-LLAVE

Poza Rica

YUCATAN

Isla Cozumel

Puerto Vallarta

Leon
Irapuato

Guanajuato

7
4

JALISCO

Guadalajara

3
Queretaro
Pachuca

Campeche

QUINTANA ROO

Chetumal

Zamora

Celaya

5

Tulancingo

Colima

Morelia

Mexico
Texcoco
8
Tlaxcala
Jalapa

Veracruz

Ciudad del Carmen

CAMPECHE

Belize City

Manzanillo

COLIMA

MICHOACAN DE OCAMPO

Toluca
2
Cuernavaca
6
Puebla
Orizaba
Cordoba

TABASCO

Coatzacoalcos
Villahermosa

BELIZE
★ **Belmopan**

Rio Balsas

Lazaro Cardenas

Chilpancingo

Minatitlan

Tuxtla Gutierrez

San Cristobal de Las Casas

CHIAPAS

Puerto Barrios

San Pedro Sula

Acapulco

GUERRERO

Oaxaca

OAXACA

Salina Cruz

Golfo de Tehuantepec

GUATEMALA
★ **Guatemala**

HONDURAS
★ **Tegucigalpa**

1. AGUASCALIENTES
2. DISTRITO FEDERAL
3. GUANAJUATO
4. HIDALGO
5. MEXICO
6. MORELOS
7. QUERETARO DE ARTEAGA
8. TLAXCALA

Tapachula

Puerto San Jose

San Salvador ★
La Union

EL SALVADOR

NIC.

0 100 200 300 Kilometers
0 100 200 300 Miles

CUBA

U.S.A.

Homestead

Key Largo

Atlantic Ocean

Key West
Marathon

Straits of Florida

Nassau
Eleuthera

New Providence

Andros Island

Exuma Cays

Cat Island

San Salvador

Gulf of Mexico

Cay Sal Bank (The Bahamas)

THE BAHAMAS

Rum Island

Great Exuma

Long Island

Crooked Island

Yucatan Channel

Minas de Matahambre

Pinar Del Rio

Mariel
Havana ★
Ciudad De La Habana
La Habana
Matanzas
Cardenas
Colon

Archipiélago De Sabana

Isabela de Sagua

Arroyos de Mantua
San Cristobal
Artemisa
Guines
Jovellanos

Villa Clara
Santa Clara
Caibarién

Archipiélago De Camagüey

Guinchos Cay (The Bahamas)

Jumentos Cays

Ragged Island Range (The Bahamas)

Acklins Island

La Fe

Guane
Pinar del Rio

Golfo de Batabanó

Surgidero de Batabanó

Matanzas

Cienfuegos
Cienfuegos

Placetas
Sancti Spiritus

Cay Lobos (The Bahamas)

Nueva Gerona

La Fe

Isla De La Juventud

Isla de la Juventud

Aguada de Pasajeros

Cayo Largo

Ciego De Ávila
Ciego de Ávila

Morón
Sancti Spiritus

Cay Santo Domingo (The Bahamas)

Great Inagua

Caribbean Sea

Archipiélago De Los Jardines De La Reina

Camagüey
Camagüey
Florida

Nuevitas

Puerto Padre

CUBA

Las Tunas
Las Tunas
Amancio

Banes
Holguin
Antilla
Holguin

Moa

Manzanillo
Bayamo
Granma
Palma Soriano
Mayari
Baracoa

Pilón
Santiago De Cuba

Santiago de Cuba

Guantanamo
Guantanamo

U.S. Naval Base Guantánamo Bay

Windward Passage

Little Cayman
Cayman Brac

HAITI

0 50 100 Kilometers
0 50 100 Miles

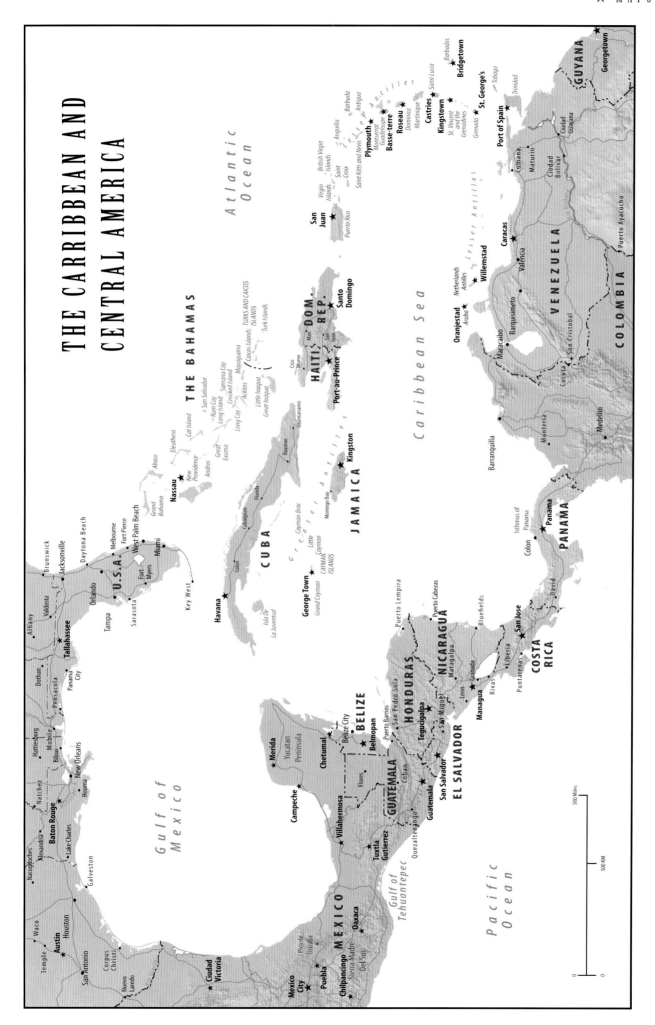

THE CARRIBBEAN AND CENTRAL AMERICA

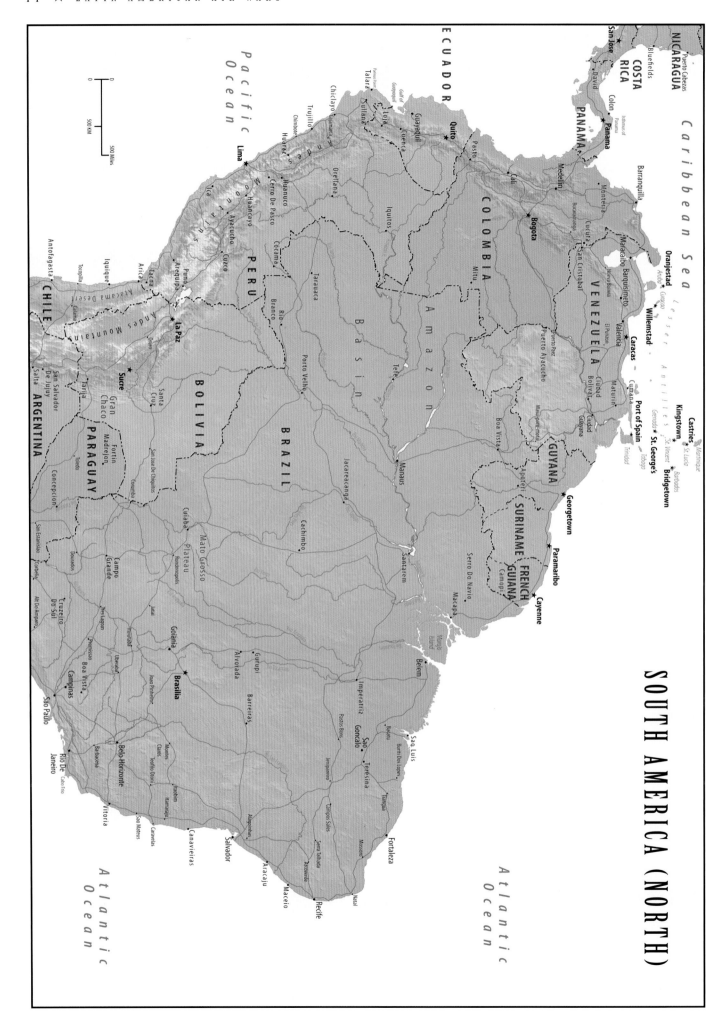

SOUTH AMERICA (NORTH)

PERU
Puno
La Paz
Arequipa
Cochabamba
Tacna
Oruro
Arica
Iquique
Tocopilla
Tarija
Calama
Antofagasta

BOLIVIA
Cuiabá
Mato Grosso Plateau
Rondonopolis
Santa Cruz
San Jose De Chiquitos
Gran Chaco
Corumba
Sucre
Fortin Madrejon
PARAGUAY
Toledo
Dourados
Concepcion
San Salvador De Jujuy
Salta
Monte Quemado
Asuncion
San Miguel De Tucuman
Coronel Oviedo
Montecarlo

Goiânia
Brasília
Paracatu
Jatai
BRAZIL
Ituiutaba
Uberaba
Promissao
Boa Vista
Bauru
Campinas
Cruzeiro Do Sul
Goio Ere
Foz Do Iguacu
Biturna

Itaobim
Montes Claros
Teofilo Otoni
Caravelas
Sao Mateus
Belo Horizonte
Vitoria
Cabo Frio
Rio De Janeiro
Sao Paulo
Registro
Curitiba
Florianopolis

Pacific Ocean

Copiapo
Catamarca
ARGENTINA
Vera
Chamical
Coquimbo
San Juan
Cerro Aconcagua
Valparaiso
Mendoza
San Luis
Santiago
Cordoba
Leones
Rosario
Rio Cuarto
Venado Tuerto
Resistencia
Saladas
Uruguaiana
Sao Sepe
Rivera
Tacuarembo
Paysandu
Durazno

Passo Fundo
Sao Luis Gonzaga
Cruz Alta
Vacaria
Jaguaruna
Porto Alegre
Capao Antonio Da Patrulha
Pelotas

Atlantic Ocean

CHILE
San Rafael
Realico
Pehuajo
Anguil
Buenos Aires
Montevideo
URUGUAY
Dolores
Olavarria
General Acha
Tres Arroyos
Bahia Blanca
Mar Del Plata

Concepcion
Chillan
Victoria
Valdivia
Zapala
Neuquen
Osorno
Puerto Montt
San Carlos de Bariloche
Esquel
Rawson
Gulf of San Matias
Valdes Penninsula
Isla Grande de Chiloe

Coihaique
Taitao Penninsula
Comodoro Rivadavia
Gulf of San Jorge

Puerto Santa Cruz
Puerto Natales
Rio Gallegos
Punta Arenas
Strait of Magellan
Tierra Del Fuego
Ushuaia

FALKLAND ISLANDS
Port Stanley

SOUTH AMERICA (SOUTH)

0   500 Miles

0   500 KM

SOUTH GEORGIA ISLAND

GLOSSARY OF TERMS

Insofar as possible, the author has honored place names, organizational titles, military ranks and events using the spelling in the language of the nation in which the term originated. While it is appreciated that this may pose a challenge in some instances to the English-language reader, the quest for accuracy of expression has dictated that the author exercise this option, as often, there are simply no English-language equivalents.

What is more, many of the terms defined herein are archaic and often not understood with precision in the nation of origin. Therefore, as part of the overall historical treatment of this vast subject, this appended Glossary is offered as a means of increasing understanding, accuracy of expression, and historical provenance.

Aéronautica Militar
Military Aeronautics, service name for the Uruguayan Army air arm during the 1920s through the 1940s

Agrupamento de Avies de Adaptação
Aircraft Familiarization Group (in effect, an Operational Training Unit), a joint U.S. Army Air Force/Brazilian Air Force organization, based at Fortaleza, Brazil circa November 1942

Agrupamiento del Norte
Northern Group, Peruvian Aeronautical Corps, a composite unit, circa 1941

Alférez
Ensign or sometime 2nd Lieutenant, a commissioned rank used in a number of Latin American air arms, including Chile, the Paraguayan Navy, and Uruguay circa 1935

Anáhuac
Popular name for a large series of modified Avro 504K trainers and general purpose biplanes built by the T.N.C.A. in Mexico during the 1920s

Arma Aérea
Air Arm, formal name of the Paraguayan military aviation during the Chaco War period

Arma Aérea Gubernista
Government Air Arm. Temporary name for the "legitimate" Paraguayan Air Force during the 1947 Civil War

Arma Aérea Revolucionaria
Revolutionary Air Arm. Temporary name for the rebel air arm created during the 1947 Paraguayan civil war

Arma de Aviação do Exército
Army Air Arm, Brazil, formal name as of 13 January, 1927

Arma de Aviación Militar
Military Aviation Arm. Short lived official name of the Mexican military aviation establishment as of 5 February 1915

Armada Aérea Nacional
National Air Fleet, Mexico, a short-lived name for the national air arm circa September 1920-

Armada Peruana
Peruvian Fleet or Peruvian Navy

Aspirante (Asp.)
Cadet or Officer-in-Training, Brazilian Air Force circa 1942-?

Aviação Brigadiana
Brigade Aviation element, Rio Grande do Sul state, planned but not actually equipped circa 1915

Aviação da Brigada Militar
Aviation of the Military Brigade, Rio Grande do Sul state, Brazil, circa 1923

Aviação Militar
Military Aviation, Brazilian Army during the 1920s and 1930s

Aviação Naval
Naval Aviation, Brazilian Navy during the 1920s and 1930s

Aviación Militar (AM) or (A.M.)
Military Aviation. Service name used by a number of Latin American air arms during the 1920s and 1930s

Aviación Naval
Service name for a number of Latin American naval aviation establishments, including Argentina as of circa 1951

Base Aeronaval de Punta Indio (BAN Punta Indio)
Naval Air Base, Argentine Navy, at Punta Indio

Bomberos
Firemen or fire department

Capitán
Captain, company grade commissioned rank in many Latin American air arms and military establishments

Cap-Av.
Captain (Aviator), Brazilian Air Force circa 1942-?

Capt. Obs.
Observer Captain, commissioned grade for an observer/gunner/bombardier, usually a non-rated pilot, in Paraguay circa 1934

CAT
China Air Transport, a CIA proprietary airline

Cia. Mexicana de Aviación
Mexican Aviation Company, created in the 1920s and more commonly known as 'Mexicana'

Club Salvadorena de Aviación Civil y Reserva
Salvadoran Civil and Reserve Air Club. A number of Latin American nations have similar organizations, which vary in character of organization and sophistication. The Salvadoran organization actually took part in light combat operations during the 1969 war with Honduras using general aviation aircraft with light bomb racks mounted, etc.

Cnel. (Coronel)
Colonel, senior field grade commissioned rank just below flag rank in most Latin American air arms and military establishments

Comando de Aviación Naval (CAN)
Naval Aviation Command, Argentina, modern service name for the Argentine Naval aviation establishment

Comisión Aeronáutica Mexicana
Mexican Aeronautical Commission, sent to Europe in September 1927 to acquire modern aircraft for the Mexican air arm

Comisión Nacional de Irrigación
National Irrigation Commission, Mexican Federal Governemnt

Companha do Contestado
Campaign of the Contested (lands) in Brazil circa 1914

Compañía de Aviación
Aviation Company, Dominican Republic circa 1946. Evolved into the modern Dominican Air Force

Constitucionalistas
Forces of Carranza, Villa and Obregón, jointly known, during the 1913-1914 period of the Mexican Revolution. Also used to describe forces of the state of São Paulo state, Brazil, during the 1930-32 civil war

Coronel (Cnel.)
Colonel (see: Cnel.)

Corpo de Aviação Naval
Brazilian Naval Aviation Corps during the 1920s and 1930s

Corps d'Aviation d'Haiti
The Haitian Air Corps, modern service name

Cpt. 1°
Abbreviation for First Captain, a Mexican commissioned grade roughly equivalent to a junior Major

Cristeros
Large, pro-Roman Catholic, largely middle-class guerrilla group in Mexico. Usually translated to mean "defenders of Christ", they attacked Regular Army garrisons, burned buildings, and once even dynamited a train, killing 100 passengers. The Cristero Rebellion was prompted by the 1926 anti-church clauses of the evolving Mexican constitution and series of laws which, beginning that year and extending into 1929, resulted in a civil war within the revolution between the Central Government and the Catholic Church in Mexico. It was finally put down after a series of conferences between the Church and the Mexican president, with the U.S. Ambassador acting as intermediary.

Cruz Roja Peruana
Peruvian Red Cross organization

Cuerpo de Aeronáutica Peruana (CAP)
Peruvian Aeronautical Corps, formal name of the combined Peruvian Army and Navy aviation establishments prior to modernization as the FAP (q.v.)

Cuerpo de Aviación
Air Corps, formal name of the Bolivian Army aviation establishment circa 1929

Cuerpo de Aviación, Ejercito de Cuba (CAEC)
Cuban Army Air Corps during the 1920s and 1930s

Cuerpo de Aviación Militar (CAM)
Military Aviation Corps. Guatemala, 1920s and 1930s.

Cuerpo de Aviadores Militares
Corps of Military Aviators, Mexico, c.May 1912. In effect, the name of the Mexican Air Force at that time.

Cuerpo Militar de Aviación
Military Air Corps, Nicaragua, circa April 1926, a relatively short-lived service name for the national air arm

Departamento de Aviación
Department of Aviation, Mexico, circa September 1920, a cabinet/ministerial level position governing military aeronautics
Destacamento Aéreo

Air Detachment, Peru circa 1932
Destacamento Amazonas Amazon Detachment, Colombian air arm, consisting of the expeditionary force led by General Alfredo Vasquez Cobo up the Amazon during the Leticia Incident with Peru

Director General de Aeronáutica
Director General of Aeronautics, a cabinet/ministerial level position found in many Latin American governments, usually held by a serving aviation officer of flag rank

Directorio Estudiantil
Student Directorate, a political movement in Cuba circa September 1933

División del Norte
Division of the North, Pancho Villa's force in Northern Mexico during the opening phase of the Mexican Revolution. It was a largely irregular force

Escola de Aviação Militar (EAM)
School of Military Aviation, Brazilian Army, formed originally 10 July 1919

Escuadrilla Aérea de la Milicia Auxiliar del Ejercito Federal
Air Squadron of the Auxiliary Militia to the Federal Army, Mexico, early revolutionary period

Escuadrilla Aeronavale de Bombardeo
Naval Aviation Bombardment Squadron, Argentine Navy circa 1951

Escuadrilla Aeronavale de Combate
Naval Aviation Combat Squadron, Argentina Navy circa 1951.

Escuadrilla de Bombardeo Independiente
Independent Bombardment Squadron, Chilean National Air Force circa 1926, equipped with Junkers R 42 tri-motor bombers – the first strategic bombing force in Latin America

Escuadrilla de Observacion Terrestre No.70
70th Land Observation Squadron, Peruvian Aeronautical Corps (CAP) circa 1941

Escuadrilla de Reconocimiento Aéreo
Air Reconnaissance Squadron, Bolivian Air Corps circa June 1932

Escuadrón Aerea Mixto
Mixed Air Squadron, Mexican Army Air Force during the Cedillo campaign

Escuadrón de Ataque y Reconocimiento (SAW)
The Guatemalan Air Force's Special Air Warfare, Attack and Reconnaissance Squadron of the 1960 period

Escuadrón Caza y Bombardeo
Fighter and Bomber Squadron, Salvadoran Air Force circa 1969. A composite unit composed of all fighter, fighter-bomber and dedicated bombing capable aircraft

Escuadrón de Bombardero Pesado
Heavy Bombardment Squadron, Mexico, circa 1925-?

Escuadrón de Caza
Fighter Squadron, Mexico circa 1925-?

Escuadrón de Observación y Bombardero Ligero
Observation and Light Bombardment Squadron, Mexico, circa 1925-?

Escuadrón de Enlace
Communications Squadron, Colombian Air Force circa 1946-1953

Escuadrón de Patrulla No.1
Patrol Squadron No.1, Colombian Air Force circa 1944, operating anti-submarine and coastal patrols from Barranquilla.

Escuadrón de Transporte
Transport Squadron. A designation used by nearly every modern Latin American air force, sometimes in conjunction with a numeric or category designator

Escuadrón de Transporte Aéreos (ETA)
Air Transport Squadron, Bolivian Air Force circa 1952

Escuadrón 'Punta de Alas'
Arrow Wings Squadron, Bolivian Army, during the Chaco War, a bomber/recon unit equipped with Junkers K 43s

Escuela de Aplicación Aeronáutica
Advanced Aeronautical School, formerly the Azcárate aircraft factory in Mexico, circa 1932-?

Escuela de Aviación Civil
Civil Aviation School. Common name for such establishments in a number of Latin American nations, usually constituted as a quasi-governmental entity, often as a direct adjunct or outgrowth of the military establishment

Escuela de Aviación Militar (EAM)
Military Aviation School as designated by a number of Latin American air arms, including Paraguay, Uruguay, Venezuela and others.

Escuela de Aviación Naval
Naval Aviation School, Argentine Navy circa 1955. Usually abbreviated ESAN

Escuela Militar de Aplicación Aeronáutica
Advanced Military Aeronautics School, Mexico circa 1925

Escuela Militar de Aspirantes
In Mexico, as of 1912-1913, the Military School of Cadets or, literally, Novices.

Escuela Militar de Aviación (EMA)
Military School of Aviation, a term used by a number of Latin American air arms to describe their training establishment, including Mexico, which established her EMA in April 1917

Escuela Nacional de Aviacion
National Aviation School, Mexico, established circa May 1916 at Balbeuna air field near Mexico City.

Escuela Politécnica
Guatemalan military academy

Esquadrilha de Bombardeio (GMAP)
Bombardment Squadron, of the GMAP, state of São Paulo, Brazil during the 1930-32 civil war

Esquadrilha de Caça
Fighter Squadron, Brazilian Air Force

Esquadrilha Azul (GMAP)
Blue Squadron, of the GMAP, state of São Paulo, Brazil during the 1930-32 civil war

Esquadrilha de Caça (GMAP)
Fighter Squadron, of the GMAP, state of São Paulo, Brazil during the 1930-32 civil war

Esquadrilha de Escola (GMAP)
School Squadron, of the GMAP, state of São Paulo, Brazil, during the 1930-32 civil war

Esquadrilha de Exploração e Observação (GMAP)
Observation and Reconnaissance Squadron, of the GMAP, state of São Paulo, Brazil during the 1930-32 civil war

Esquadrilha Vermelha (GMAP)
Red Squadron, of the GMAP, state of São Paul, Brazil, during the 1930-32 civil war

Escuadrilla del Ebano
Literally, the Black Squadron, Mexico, early revolutionary period

Escuadrilla de Aplicación de la Escuela de Aviación
Advanced Squadron of the Aviation School, Chilean National Air Force circa 1927-?

Estancias
Ranches or estates common through Latin America in Spanish -speaking nations

Fábrica de Cartuchos do Realengo
Royal Cartridge Factory, Brazil, circa 1914

Fabrica Militar de Avions (F.M.A.)
Military Aircraft Factory, Argentina, later Industria Aeronáutica (I.Ae.)

Ferrocarril Central
Central Railroad, Mexico in the 1920s and 1930s

Flotilla Aérea del Ejercito Constitucionalista
Air Flotilla of the Constitutional Army, Mexico, during the early revolutionary period

Flotilla de Operaciones Numero 1
Number 1 Operation Flotilla, Mexican air arm circa 1917-1918

Flotilla de Operaciones Numero 2
Number 2 Operations Flotilla, Mexican air arm circa March 1918

Flotilla de Operaciones Numero 3
Number 3 Operations Flotilla, Mexican air arm circa March 1919-?

Flotilla de Operaciones Numero 4
Number 4 Operations Flotilla, Mexican air arm circa April 1919-?

Flotilla do Amazonas
Amazon Flotilla, Brazilian Navy circa 1924-25

Força Aérea Brasileira
Brazilian Air Force, modern service name, usually abbreviated FAB

Força Pública de São Paulo (F.P.S.P.)
São Paulo State Public Force, the state military force in the 1920s, which included an aviation element.

Fortín
A comparatively small, modestly fortified strong point, usually named, and used by both Bolivia and Paraguay during the Chaco War

Fuerza Aérea Argentina
Argentine Air Force, modern service name, usually abbreviated FAA

Fuerza Aérea Boliviana
Bolivian Air Force, modern service name, usually abbreviated FAB

Fuerza Aérea de Chile
Chilean Air Force, modern service name, usually abbreviated FAC, FACH or FACh

Fuerza Aérea Colombiana
Colombian Air Force, modern service name, usually abbreviated FAC

Fuerza Aérea Costarricense
Costa Rican Air Force, used briefly circa 1955

Fuerza Aérea Dominicana
Dominican Air Force, modern service name, usually abbreviated FAD

Fuerza Aérea Ecuatoriana
The Ecuadorian Air Force, modern service name, usually abbreviated FAE

Fuerza Aérea Guatemalteca
Guatemalan Air Force, modern service name, usually abbreviated FAG

Fuerza Aérea Hondureña
The Honduran Air Force, modern service name, usually abbreviated FAH

Fuerza Aerea de Liberación
The Liberation Air Force of the Cuban expatriate Brigada 2506 during the Bay of Pigs invasion period

Fuerza Aérea Mexicana
The Mexican Air Force, modern service name, usually abbreviated FAM, commencing 1927-28

Fuerza Aérea Militar
Military Air Force. The short-lived name for the Costa Rican air force circa 1948.

Fuerza Aérea Nacional
National Air Force. Formal name used by the Chilean and Mexican Air Forces (circa 1928-29) at certain intervals in their history.

Fuerza Aérea de Nicaragua
The Nicaraguan Air Force. This is a descriptor used twice during the history of Nicaraguan service aviation. During the Sandinista era, the service name was formally changed to Fuerza Aérea Sandinista. Usually abbreviated FAN (or FAS)

Fuerza Aérea del Ejercito de la Revolucion Americana
Air Force of the American Revolutionary Army, the formal name for the still-born air force of the Caribbean Legion of the 1940s and 1950s. Sometimes abbreviated as FAERA

Fuerza Aérea Revolucionaria
The Cuban Revolutionary Air Force, from 1959 under Castro. Usually abbreviated FAR

Fuerza Aérea Salvadoreña
Salvadoran Air Force, modern service name, usually abbreviated FAS. More recently, also abbreviated as FAES

Fuerzas Aéreas Venezolanas
The Venezuelan Air Forces, modern service name, usually abbreviated FAV

Fuerza Aeronaval No.1
1st Naval Aviation Force, Argentina Navy circa 1951. Roughly equivalent to a U.S. Navy Fleet Air Wing

Gabinete de Fotogrametria Aérea (G.F.A.)
Laboratory of Aerial Photography and Mapping, a specialized unit of the Chilean National Air Force circa 1926

General brigadier
Brigadier General, Mexico and elsewhere

General de brigada (Gen. Bgd.)
General of Brigade. Roughly equivalent to U.S. Major General

General de division
Division General, roughly equivalent to U.S. Lieutenant General, Mexico and elsewhere

Grupamento de Avi_es de Caça
Fighter Aircraft Group, Brazilian Air Force circa August 1942

Grupo Aéreo de Caza
Fighter Group. Used by a number of Latin American air forces, usually with a numeric designator, but seldom the same strength composition as a U.S. or British Group

Grupo de Aviación No.1 and No.3
1st and 3rd Aviation Groups, Chilean National Air Force circa 1926-27

Grupo de Bombardeio Médio
Medium Bombardment Group, Brazilian Air Force as of 1942

Grupo de Combate
Combat Group, Salvadoran Air Force circa 1969. Essentially, senior organization for all subordinate units with aircraft capable of being committed to combat operations. Term also used to describe the combat element of the Bolivian national air arm as of circa 1928-?

Grupo de Esquadrilhas de Aviação
Brazilian Army aviation circa 1922, first tactical organization. Literally, the Grupo of Aviation Squadrons

Grupo Misto de Aviação
Mixed Aviation Group, Brazilian Army circa 1932. These units varied in size, mission and composition Grupo Misto de Aviação da Força Pública de Estado (GMAP) Mixed Aviation Group, State Public Force, state of São Paulo, Brazil during the 1930-32 civil war

Grupo 1 de Caza-Bombardeo (CB-1)
Argentine Air Force 1st Fighter-Bomber Group circa the early 1960s, equipped with North American F-86F Sabres at the time

Guardia Civil
Civil Guard, Peru, long-standing para-military national police force

Guardiamarina
Equivalent of Midshipman in a number of Latin American navies

Insurrecto
Literally, a rebel

Jefe del Departamento de Aviación
Chief of the Department of Aviation, Mexico, during the 1920s

LATN Linea Aérea Transporte Nacional
The Paraguayan national air line operated as part of the Paraguayan Air Force for part of its existence

Legalista
Common term used to describe Brazilian Federal forces during the 1930-32 civil war period

Legión Aérea Extranjero
Foreign Air Legion, title applied to foreign pilots who volunteered to fly for Paraguay during the Chaco War. Unclear whether official or colloquial

Línea Aérea Nacional (LAN)
National Air Line of Chile, created as part of the National Air Force

Los cinco primeros
Literally, "the first five," a phrase used to describe what were believed to be the first five trained Mexican pilots c.January 1913, graduates of the Moisant School.

Maestranza de Aviación
Aviation Arsenal or Workshops, Chilean National Air Force circa 1928-?

May-Av.
Major (Aviator), Brazilian Air Force

Mayor
Major, usually an Army, Air Force or Marine Corps officer rank in Latin American military establishments, similar in grade to the U.S. equivalent.

Mayor P.A.
Major, Pilot Aviator. Mexico and several other Latin American air arms at different times

Mestizo
A term used to describe a person of mixed Spanish and Amerindian blood. Thought to have originated during the period of Spanish rule in much of Latin America

Movimiento Nacional Revolucionaria (MNR)
National Revolutionary Movement, Bolivia, circa 1949-52

Movimiento Revolucionaria Dominicano (MRD)
Dominican Revolutionary Movement. One of the seeds of the Caribbean Legion of the 1940s and 1950s

Palácio do Governo (Catete)
Brazilian Presidential palace

Partido Revolucionaria Dominicano
Dominican Revolutionary Party. One of the seeds of the Caribbean Legion of the 1940s and 1950s

Porfiriato
The period during which Porfirio Díaz was president of Mexico. Variously measured, it is usually described as lasting until 1911 and the commencement of the Revolution

Primeira Esquadrilha
First Squadron, Brazilian Naval aviation circa 1924

Primeiro-Tenente Observador
First Lieutenant Observer, Brazilian Army aviation circa 1922

Primera Escuadrilla de Caza
1st Fighter Squadron, Paraguayan Air Arm circa 1929-?

Primera Escuadrilla de Reconocimiento y Bombardeo
First Reconnaissance and Bombardment Squadron, Paraguay circa Chaco War era

Quartel
Antique (old) version of cuartel, usually meaning a barracks or base.

Rurales
Term used to describe local militia groups organized in Mexico in the 1920s and 1930, later formalized into a paramilitary organization

SAHSA
Servicio Aéreo de Honduras, S.A., until it ceased operations in January 1994, the national flag carrier airline of Honduras

Sargento Mayor
Sergeant Major, the most senior Non-Commissioned grade/rank in many Latin American service branches

Seccion de Caza Tactico
Honduran Air Force circa 1962, a Tactical Fighter Section or flight. Typically smaller than a Squadron (Escuadron) in strength and composition

Seccion de Coordinación Aéreo
Honduran Air Force circa 1962, a Liaison Section or flight

Seccion de Helicoptero
Honduran Air Force circa 1962, a Helicopter Section

Seccion de Transporte Aéreo
Honduran Air Force c.1962, an Air Transport Section or flight. Typically smaller than a Squadron (Escuadron) in strength and composition

Secretaria de Comunicaciones y Obras Publicas (SCOP)
Secretary of Communications and Public Works. A national-level ministry in Mexico which operated aircraft in the performance of the official duties of the agency, and still does

Secretario de Guerra y Marina
Secretary of War and Marine, cabinet/ministerial government post overseeing all military and naval affairs, Mexico, circa 1929-

SEDTA (Sociedad Ecuatoriana de Transportes Aéreos, S.A.)
Ecuadorian Air Transport Company pre-1941, formed by German interests

Segunda Esquadrilha
Second Squadron, Brazilian Naval aviation circa 1924

Segunda Escuadrilla de Reconocimiento y Bombardeo
Second Reconnaissance and Bombardment Squadron, Paraguay, circa Chaco War era

Semana de Aviación
Aviation Week, an annual event in Mexico commencing in December 1929

Serie A
Series A biplane, an indigenous Mexican production design built by the Tallares Nacional de Construcciónes Aeronautica (T.N.C.A.) in the 1920s

Serie H
Series H monoplane, an indigenous Mexican production design built by the T.N.C.A. in the 1920s

Serviço Geográfico do Exercito
Army Cartographic Service, Brazilian Army circa 1919-?

Sgto.
Abbreviation for Sargento or Sergeant, a common Non-Commissioned Officer rank in many Latin American air arms

Sub. Of. MAM
Non-Commissioned Officer, Aviation Maintenance Mate, Paraguayan Navy circa 1947

Sub.Ofc.
Non-Commissioned Officer, Peru circa 1932

Sub Oficial (P.A.M.)
Non-Commissioned Officer Military Aviation Pilot, non-com rank in Uruguayan air arm as of 1935

Subteniente (Sub.Tte.)
Sub Lieutenant. Roughly equivalent to 2nd Lieutenant in U.S. services

Tallares Generales de Aeronautica
General Aviation Factory or Works, Mexico circa May 1941, formerly the Canadian Car and Foundry (CCF) factory there.

Tallares Nacionales de Construcciónes Aeronáuticas (T.N.C.A.)
National Aeronautical Construction Workshops, Mexico. Designed and built a series of indigenous designs during the 1920s.

Teco-Teco
Brazilian familiar nickname for the Piper L-4 aircraft used by the 1.ª Esquadrilla de Ligação e Observação in Italy during World War Two.

Ten-Av.
Lieutenant (Aviator), Brazilian Air Force circa 1942.

Tenente-Aviador
Lieutenant Aviator (Pilot), Brazilian Army aviation circa 1924

Teniente (Tte.)
Lieutenant. Common company grade commissioned rank in many Latin American air arms and military establishments

Tercera Escuadra Aeronaval, Escuadrilla de Ataque
Literally, Attack Squadron of the 3rd Naval Aviation Fleet Squadron, (Argentine Navy). However, in effect, more akin to the U.S. relationship between a Group and a subordinate Squadron within the Group.

Tte. Cnel.
Lieutenant Colonel. Field grade commissioned rank common in many Latin American air arms and military establishments

Tte. Comandante
Lieutenant Commander, commissioned grade Peru circa 1932

Tte. de Corbeta
Corvette Lieutenant, an Argentine Navy commissioned rank circa 1955

Tte. de Fragata
Frigate Lieutenant. A Paraguayan Naval commissioned rank circa 1947

Tte. de Navio PAN
Naval Lieutenant, Naval Aviation Pilot, Paraguay circa 1947

Tte. P.A.
Teniente (Lieutenant) Pilot Aviator. Mexico and various other Latin American air arms at different times

Tte. 1º
1st Lieutenant, a common junior commissioned rank in many Latin American air arms

Tte. 1º PAM
1st Lieutenant, Military Aviation Pilot, a common junior commissioned rank in some Latin American air arms, especially during the 1930s and 1940s

Tte. 2º
2nd Lieutenant, a common junior commissioned rank in many Latin American military establishments

Undecima Escuadrilla de Caza
11th Fighter Squadron, Paraguayan Air Arm, circa 1933-?

UsBaTu
United States-Brazilian Training Unit circa 1943, formed for anti-submarine training.

Vicealmirante
Vice Admiral, a flag rank common in a number of Latin American naval establishments

Vicecomodoro
Vice Commodore, an Argentine Air Force (not Naval) rank circa 1955

1ª Divisão de Observação
1st Observation Division, Brazilian Navy circa 1932.

1ª Esquadrilha de Aperfeiçoamento
1st Advanced Training Squadron, Brazilian Army aviation circa 1924

1ª Esquadrilha de Bombardeio
1st Bombardment Squadron, Brazilian Army aviation, first such unit designated as such circa 1922

1ª Esquadrilha de Caça
1st Fighter Squadron, Brazilian Army aviation, first such unit designated as such circa 1922

1ª Escuadrilla Aeronaval de Ataque
Argentine Naval aviation unit, the 1st Naval Attack Squadron, somewhat smaller than a full Escuadron (Squadron also). Operated Grumman F9F-2 Panthers and other types from the 1950s and 1960s

1.ªEsquadrilla de Ligação e Observação
1st Liaison and Observation Squadron, Brazilian Air Force. Served in Italy in World War Two in direct support of the Brazilian Infantry Division there flying Piper L-4s

1er Escuadrilla del 1er Regimiento Aéreo
1st Squadron of the 1st Air Regiment, Mexico circa 1929-?

1º Escuadron de Bombardero Ligero
1st Light Bombardment Squadron, Colombian Air Force circa 1953 equipped with North American B-25Js

1º Escuadron de Caza
1st Fighter Squadron, Colombian Air Force circa 1946-1953 equipped with Republic P-47Ds.

1º Grupo de Aviação Constitucionalista
1st Constitutionalist Aviation Group, state of São Paulo during the 1930-32 civil war

1.º Grupo de Caça (1.º GAvC)
1st Fighter Group, Brazilian Air Force. In actuality, closer in size to a reinforced USAAF squadron and often translated as 1st Fighter Squadron. Served following training during World War Two in Italy and still exists lineally today.

1.º Grupo de Patrulla
1st Patrol Group, Brazilian Air Force, based at Galeão Air Base, near Rio de Janeiro with Consolidated PBY-5 Catalinas as of 1943. In actuality, more akin to a USAAF squadron in size

1.º Grupo Misto de Aviação
1st Mixed Aviation Group, Brazilian Air Force after October 1942

1º Regimento de Aviação (1.º R.Av.)
1st Aviation Regiment, Brazilian Army as of late 1932 through at least 1941

1º Ten-Av.
1st Lieutenant (Aviator), Brazilian Air Force

2.º Corpo de Base Aérea (2.º CBAé)
2nd Air Base Corps, Brazilian Army aviation circa 1941, headquartered at São Paulo

2º Regimiento Aéreo
2nd Air Regiment, Mexican Army Aviation circa 1931-39

2.ªZona Aérea
Second Air Zone (headquartered at Natal, Brazil), Brazilian Air Force, as of October 1942-.

3ª Companhia Provisoria de Parque de Aviação
3rd Supply Company, Aviation Depot, Brazilian Army aviation circa 1922

3ª Esquadrilha de Observação
3rd Observation Squadron, Brazilian Army aviation circa 1922

3.ªRegião Militar
3rd Military Region, Brazilian Army circa 1941, headquartered at Curitiba

3.º Regimento de Aviação (3.º R. Av.)
3rd Aviation Regiment, Brazilian Army aviation headquartered at Pôrto Alegre as of 1941.

4.º Corpo de Base Aérea (4.º CBAé)
4th Air Base Corps, Brazilian Army aviation circa 1941, headquartered at Belo Horizonte

4ª D.E.B.
Brazilian Navy aviation unit equipped with Fairey Gordons as of 1932-?

4.º Grupo de Bombardeio Médio
4th Medium Bombardment Group, Brazilian Air Force, headquartered at Fortaleza, Brazil circa November 1942. In actuality, in size about that of a U.S. squadron

5.ª Regiao Militar
5th Military Region, Brazilian Army, circa 1941

5.º Regimento de Aviacao (5.º R. Av.)
5th Aviation Regiment, Brazilian Army aviation headquartered at Curitiba circa 1941

6.º Corpo de Base Aérea (6.º CBAé)
6th Air Base Corps, Brazilian Army aviation circa 1941 headquartered at Fortaleza

7.º Corpo de Base Aérea (7.º CBAé)
7th Air Base Corps, Brazilian Army aviation circa 1941 headquartered at Belém

8.º Corpo de Base Aérea (8.º CBAé)
8th Air Base Corps, Brazilian Army aviation circa 1941 headquartered at Mato Grosso

9.º Corpo de Base Aérea (9.º CBAé)
9th Air Base Corps, Brazilian Army aviation circa October 1942 headquartered at Natal

11.º Corpo de Base Aérea (11.º CBAé)
11th Air Base Corps, Brazilian Air Force, circa October 1942, headquartered at Salvador, Brazil. In effect, a form of Air Base Wing incorporating all of the aviation assets in that area

12.º Corpo de Base Aérea
As above, headquartered near Rio de Janeiro as of November 1942. Evolved into the 3.º Grupo de Bombardeo Medio (3rd Medium Bombardment Group) by August 1944, Brazilian Air Force

The Mexican Revolutionary Period

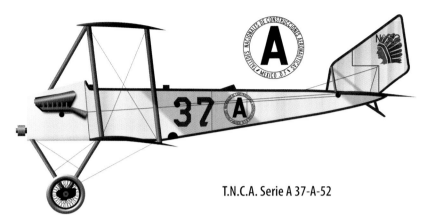

T.N.C.A. Serie A 37-A-52

To the distant observer, the chaotic events of the Mexican Revolutionary period must appear a historical blur. Filled with ever-changing alliances and intrigue, this period – forming the longest chapter in our accompanying on-line downloads – is presented first because it involved the earliest uses of aircraft in warfare in the region and, secondly, because the sheer breadth of the internal struggles spanned and were continuing throughout the period that other, more clearly defined events, were unfolding elsewhere in Latin America.

Although an oversimplification, for the purposes of this work the classic revolutionary period can be divided into a number of successive, distinct epochs. Perhaps not surprisingly, the aviation component of each of these closely paralleled the evolution of aeronautics as it advanced world-wide, improvements and applications not lost upon the various factions that ultimately acquired and employed aircraft.

At the outset, the established Mexican Army, at the behest of none other than the legendary President Porfirio Díaz, and his revolutionary successor, President Madero, after witnessing demonstrations of pioneering aircraft and their potential as weapons of war, enabled the formation of one of the earliest military aviation establishments in Latin America. Following the social customs of the time, a number of Army officers were selected to be sent to France for training, and orders were placed for various aircraft, both in France and the U.S.

Not surprisingly, the earliest aircraft sought were variants of the capable Blériot XI and a U.S. improvement, the Moisant monoplane. However, representations were also made to the Wrights via an agency, as the stature of the Wright name and aircraft line could not be ignored.

With this beginning, the first period of aviation during the Mexican revolutionary period commenced, and lasted roughly from 1911 to 1918. Almost from the beginning, both Mexican Federal as well as insurrectionist forces engaged foreigners, along with aircraft of obscure parentage, to undertake reconnaissance and, gradually, harassment and light attack duties. These were amongst the first such sorties in aviation history, and although conducted under the most primitive conditions imaginable and on a basis that might be characterized at best as "occasional," they nonetheless represented the realization that both established military forces and insurrectionists alike recognized the value of the new science and intended to capitalize upon it at every opportunity.

This first period saw several specific uses of aircraft that stand out historically. First, railroads, of which Mexico had a fairly well established system north of the capital by 1911, were key to the success of the Federal forces, and as a result, train escort by aircraft became one of the most frequent – and important - missions assigned to the infant service. The Mexican Federal forces also developed the use of aerial bombs and bomb racks for their aircraft and, although often cited as making use of such weapons for the first time in aviation history, in fact it might be better expressed as making practical and frequent use of these for the first time.

The period also saw the establishment of one of the first permanent military aviation schools in the hemisphere, which has evolved into the present day Mexican Air Force training establishment, one of the oldest and continuously operating on earth.

Meanwhile, as the Revolution continued to expand and contort, regional Federal commanders found it expedient to hire their own airmen to mimic the success they perceived elsewhere. As a result, a remarkable array of airmen and aircraft were introduced into the country, and perhaps most famous of all was Didier Masson and his 1911 Martin pusher which eventually gained the name Sonora. This aircraft and its assorted crew became immortalized as the weapon that carried out the first aerial attack on surface warships in the history of warfare and, while the results may not have been decisive, they shortly became the stuff of legend and are detailed at length in the main text.

Meanwhile, the charismatic Pancho Villa, who early on had headed the so-called *División del Norte*, part of the Federal forces, had also decided that an aviation corps might be useful, and gradually recruited his own troop of mercenaries to act as scouts for his highly mobile and far-ranging forces. The activities of these adventurers, and the odd aircraft they brought to the conflict, are also described in detail, for the first time, in the main text to be found on-line.

Finally, in February 1915, the Central Government acted to formalize the diverse aviation elements under Federal control, and established the *Arma de Aviación Militar*, and the modern-day Mexican Air Force (*Fuerza Aérea Mexicana*) dates its creation from this organization.

The first epoch is also replete with legends, which are discussed in detail in the on-line text. These include the alleged introduction into the conflict of Wright Model L aircraft, and the oft-repeated account of the aerial "dog-fight" – supposedly the first in aviation history – between mercenaries Philip Rader and Dean Ivan Lamb near Naco in 1913. The period also saw the first manifestations of national insignia on Federal aircraft.

The second phase of the Revolution may be said to have started in 1917-1918, when the victorious Carranza forces attempted to consolidate power – only to be met by armed resistance almost at once. This phase saw the gradual replacement of the pioneering aircraft of the first phase, which had stood up remarkably well to the rigors of field use, by purpose-built, imported aircraft, and indigenously designed and fabricated aircraft turned out by the *Tallares Nacionales de Construcciónes Aeronáuticas* (*TNCA*).

The *TNCA* aircraft are unique in aviation history in that they were the first production aircraft designed, built and fielded for combat use in Latin America, and were a direct response to Mexico's desire to become self-sufficient in the supply of aerial weapons of war. Consisting of several significant *Serie*, they were organized into tactical units and, with a slowly growing number of indigenously trained crews, soon brought themselves to bear against various insurgent elements throughout the country.

The other principal development of the second phase was the acquisition by the Mexican Federal forces of 13 French-built Farman F 50 twin-engine heavy bombers in 1920, the first such aircraft acquired, operated, and used operationally in Latin America. It is a credit to the crews that they were able to assemble and make operational such comparatively large aircraft in such short order, especially in view of the quite small and modestly powered aircraft they had experienced before.

The third phase of aviation's involvement in the Revolution was one of the longest and most difficult to follow, lasting from the early 1920s through 1924. During this period, the start that the Federal forces had made in establishing the framework of a permanent service began to bear fruit, and acceptance by the more conventional ground and naval forces, based primarily on their modest but highly visible involvement in the first and second phases was grudgingly realized. By this time, the *TNCA* series of aircraft had been all but worn out by field operations, and production had switched to a non-authorized copy of the Avro 504K known locally as the *Anahuac*, which quickly became numerically the most significant aircraft in the Mexican arsenal. These were augmented by more capable, U.S. built variants of the First World War vintage de Havilland D.H.4, as well as small numbers of other exotic aircraft, including Ansaldo SVA variants, as well as various French and even one or two German aircraft designs.

Another phase, which may be regarded as the fourth, commenced in 1926 and 1927, when the long-suffering Yaqui Indians in Sonora State once again took up arms against the Central Government, followed almost immediately by the so-called *Cristeros* movement. This phase saw yet more new equipment introduced into the Mexican Federal

arsenal to deal specifically with the needs of internal policing, and these included Douglas O-2C and British-built Bristol F.2B Fighters, some of the last examples built, as well as two little-known Bristol Boarhounds, as well as minor types.

By 1927, aircraft as weapons of war had come a long way since the hand-held grenades and pipe bombs lobbed by the pioneers of 1911. The Government was once again experimenting with indigenous designs, a few of which reached small-scale production but achieved only limited tactical success, leading to the Federal Government once again going to foreign sources for capable aircraft. Shortly thereafter, in 1928 and 1929, the so-called *Rebelion Escobarista* erupted and, once again, both Federal and insurrectionist elements made use of aircraft that operated over much of the northern regions of the country.

The introduction of state-of-the-art Vought O2U-2M Corsairs and additional, modernized Douglas O-2M reconnaissance bombers, into the Federal forces, with license-built variants of the O2U to follow, finally standardized the established air force on two capable types. Meanwhile, the Escobar forces introduced the most bizarre array of aircraft imaginable to support its efforts, and these are detailed in the on-line text for the first time.

The final phase of the Revolution included the *Cedillo* Rebellion in 1938 and 1939. By this time, the Mexican Federal air arm was very well established in dual regimental strength and, besides operating significant numbers of Vought and Azcárate-built variants of the Corsair, surviving Douglas O-2Ms and a hodge-podge of lesser types, had also acquired examples of the last of the great Vought biplane series, the V-99M Corsair. These were pitted in a short, bitter, campaign, against an extraordinary collection of aircraft brought together by the ambitious Cedillo, but which saw rather less involvement than he might have wished. It also saw the first introduction of the use of camouflage to Mexican tactical aircraft, and close coordination with land forces, hammered out as the result of the long campaigns of the previous phases of the revolution.

LEFT: Juan Guillermo Villasaña, a name that figured prominently in Mexican military aeronautics between 1913 and 1918. He was the first "bombardier" in Mexico, and later became director of the EMA (Escuela de Aviación Militar). His contributions to aviation during the revolutionary period are the "stuff of legend." (Ing. Jose Villela)

ABOVE: Los cinco Mexicanos, the first five Mexicans to be trained specifically as military aviators, at the Moisant School on Long Island, New York. From left to right, they were Alberto Salinas Carranza, Gustavo Salinas Camiña, Juan Pablo Aldasoro Suárez, Horacio Ruiz Gaviño and Eduardo Aldasoro Suárez. The Moisant-built Blériot XI behind them is similar to the machines with which they returned to Mexico. All five became prominent in the events of the Revolution. (Francisco Obregon Ortiz)

LEFT: One of two Moisant-built Blériot XI copies, a single seater with a 50hp engine, flown by John Worden and Francisco Alvarez for the Huerta forces against Orozco in Chihuahua in 1911. These were the first aviators to actually take part in warfare in the Western Hemisphere. (Ing. Jose Villela)

LEFT: One of the most famous aircraft in both Mexican and world aviation history, the Martin Model 1912 Pusher named Sonora. At left, its first combat pilot, Didier Masson and, on the undercarriage horizontal cross member just behind the feet of the man on the right, the crude bomb racks, fashioned to carry out aerial bombing attacks on Federal warships at Guaymas in May 1913. (Albert Leach via Greg Whipple)

BELOW: The former Buen Tono Blériot XI acquired for use by the Escuadrilla Aérea de la Milicia Auxiliar del Ejército Federal in 1913. Radically under-powered for conditions at Mexico City, Federal aviator Miguel Lebrija was apparently finally able to get it airborne. (via Santiago Flores Ruiz)

ABOVE: The Martin Model 1912 Pusher Sonora enjoyed a rather longer than might be expected service life with the Carranza forces. Here it is seen much later in its Mexican sojourn, probably after one of several crashes, reconfigured with a Curtiss-style forward elevator, the forward vertical fin having been deleted. (via Ing. Jose Villela)

LEFT: One of the durable Moisant Military Monoplanes being flown for the Carranza forces by W. Leonard Bonney. These are the first aircraft believed to have employed markings of any kind in Latin American air warfare. They carried the name of the force, División del Norte in a half-circle script on the rudder. (Aerial Age, January 3, 1916 via Santiago Flores)

RIGHT: One of the Moisant Military Monoplanes (also known as Moisant Tandem Military Monoplanes) acquired by the Constitucionalista forces in 1914. A true hybrid, the aircraft employed features of Morane-Saulnier influence with Blériot style undercarriage.

LEFT: At least one of the Moisant Military Monoplanes survived the first round of revolutionary action in Mexico to gain the country's first true national markings. The aircraft appears to have had a name or number on the fuselage, and some additional markings on the rudder. (Ing. Jose Villela).

RIGHT: A single advanced Wright Model HS was amongst a group of miscellaneous Wright designs acquired by the Pancho Via forces in Mexico commencing late 1914. Often reported in error as Wright Model L's, a 1916 design, the Model HS did see limited action. (via Dr. Wes Smith)

BELOW: A copy of an telegram that J.S. Berger sent to an early U.S. aviator named Day on April 10, 1915, asking him to sign on to fly Curtiss aircraft in Mexico for the Villa forces. (via Dr. Wes Smith)

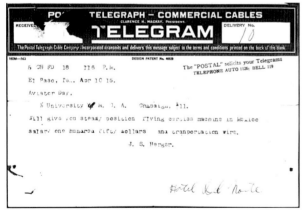

ABOVE: This is almost certainly the biplane built from the remains of the Moisant Military Monoplane No.3 at Puebla in 1915 by Francisco Santarini. It has been variously described as the Biplano Santarini or the Biplano Militar No.1. Note the characteristic Blériot style undercarriage, fuselage, and engine cowl. This served as essentially the prototype for the indigenous T.N.C.A. Serie A biplane series that followed in 1917-1918. (via Ing. Jose Villela).

RIGHT: Probably the most modern aircraft to see service in Mexico during the early revolutionary period, the first Martin Model TT tractor biplane was delivered new to the Villa forces in June 1915 by William A. "Sailor" Lamkey and his mechanic. (Author's Collection)

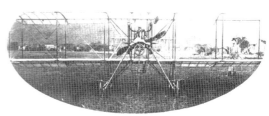

ABOVE: Photos of the little-known Kirkham Biplane are rare. Here, a head-on-view of one of the pushers reveals a rather small, compact machine, one of which apparently reached Mexico during the initial revolutionary period. (Aerial Age, 1911)

ABOVE: Often described in error as a look-alike Curtiss Model D, U.S. soldier-of-fortune Philip Rader flew bombing and reconnaissance missions for the revolutionary forces of Maytorena near Naco in September 1914 with this Christofferson pusher biplane. (via Hector Davila Cornejo)

BELOW: The duo of Francisco Santarini and Juan Guillermo Villasaña were seemingly everywhere in early Mexican aviation. Here, Villasaña in shop clothes poses with one of the long Anahuac propellers. These were locally designed and fabricated for the high-altitude Mexican conditions, for mounting on the indigenous Aztatl engines. (via Ing. Jose Villela).

ABOVE: Although the approximately 80hp indigenous Aztatl engine was credited to the Mexican engineer, Francisco Santarini, seen here, he had worked with the Anzani engine firm previously, and undoubtedly incorporated features of that manufacturer. (via Ing. Jose Villela).

ABOVE: The fuselage of this T.N.C.A. Serie A, serial number '3', is shown undergoing field maintenance with one of the specially equipped rail cars. The rail car is still marked with the insignia of the Division del Norte emblem on its door, and was used to support a number of early Mexican aviation units while on deployment. This aircraft appears to be fitted with a 150hp Hispano-Suiza engine. (via Santiago Flores)

ABOVE, RIGHT, ABOVE RIGHT :
Three views of T.N.C.A. Serie A
37-A-52, equipped with a 150hp
Hispano-Suiza engine. The only
concession to national markings
appears to have been the tri-colors
of the republic on the ailerons.
Note on the left side the "indian
chief" image on the rudder, and the
full serial is scripted at the base of
the vertical fin. The edges of the
fuselage, rudder, and elevators also
appear to have been painted. The
arrangement of the bomb racks,
vertically, for six of the locally made
weapons is noteworthy.
(National Archives)

ABOVE: The production T.N.C.A. Serie A biplanes were joined in operations in the field with Mexican forces in March 1919 for the first time by the new Serie H parasol monoplanes.
Here, 12-H-67 displays the rather frail construction of these aircraft, also powered by the 80hp Aztatl engine, but now wearing tri-color rudder stripes and the "shield" style national insignia under each
outer wing in rather small scale. (Ing. Jose Villela)

LEFT: Very possibly the oldest indigenously built aircraft surviving in Latin America, here is T.N.C.A. Serie H 12-H-67 once again, preserved as of 1980 at the Palacio de las Deportes in Mexico City. The color scheme is believed to be accurate.
(Santiago Flores Ruiz)

LEFT: Operating conditions in the field in Mexico resulted in frequent accidents and this T.N.C.A. Serie A was no exception. It bears a seldom seen variation of the shield-style national insignia.
(Author's Collection)

ABOVE: One of the first Mexican service aircraft to bear the now familiar triangular national insignia, here is T.N.C.A. Serie H 12-H-67, veteran of the revolution, as it appeared in 1920.
(via Hector Davila Cornejo)

RIGHT: A 1917 Villasaña design of the T.N.C.A. for an 80hp "scout" type, the so-called Microplano. It was the first such aircraft designed and built exclusively in Latin America. It had an all-steel tube structure and was coded 1-C-31, but it did not go into even limited production.
(via Ing. Jose Villela).

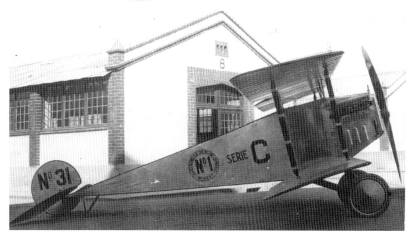

ABOVE: A survivor of the first phase of the Mexican revolution, one of the Moisant Military Monoplanes, poses between two early indigenously designed and built aircraft sometime before 1920. On the left is the rare T.N.C.A. Serie B parasol and, on the extreme right, the rare Christofferson Tractor. (via Ing. Jose Villela).

LEFT: The Mexican Farman F 50s soon came to represent the power of the Central Government. During the course of their service, they wore a variety of color schemes. This example is seen arriving at Guadalajara, Jalisco in April 1923. (via Santiago Flores)

ABOVE: By 1920, the Mexican authorities realized that the rather frail and under-powered aircraft being produced by the T.N.C.A. would need to be supplemented by more capable foreign designs. One of the first to be procured, representing a quantum leap for Mexican aircrews, were at least 13 large Farman F 50Bn2s from France, which started arriving in May 1920. (National Archives via Santiago Flores)

LEFT: None other than General Alvaro Obregón himself, center, poses with Capt.'s Ascension Santana and Rafael Ponce de Leon beside one of the prized Farman F 50s at Irapuato in 1924 during the actions against the Huerta insurgency. (via Santiago Flores)

ABOVE: Serialed 9-F-93, this Farman F 50 saw active service based at Irapuato in 1924 during the de la Huertista period of the Revolution. Two De Havilland D.H.4Bs can be seen in the background. (via Santiago Flores)

LEFT: Amongst the first foreign aircraft acquired by Mexico during 1920-21 were four examples of the little-known Brown Special, including 38-A-135 shown here. Powered by 120hp Hall-Scott engines, they were often mistakenly identified as Curtiss JN-4s, but were a much smaller design overall. Two of them gave good service well into 1929. (via Ing. Jose Villela).

BELOW: Two of the surviving Brown Specials were rebuilt locally after a hangar fire, and operated as trainers for a considerable time known only by individual names. This one, shown circa 1923, was named "Nenette" in script on either side of the fuselage, and appears to have had a highly polished radiator frame. (Tohtli 1923 via Santiago Flores)

ABOVE: A local derivative of the Avro 504 with a redesigned and strengthened undercarriage, the Avro Anáhuac series gave very good service through the 1920s, and examples were often armed and used in combat. (via Hector Davila Cornejo)

ABOVE/RIGHT: The first genuine fighter aircraft ever acquired for use in Mexico, a single Ansaldo A.1 Ballila, coded 1-D-79 served briefly between about 1921 and 1923. (Tohtli via Santiago Flores)

Ansaldo SVA 10, coded '2-D-80'

ABOVE: The acquisition of European combat aircraft enabled the Mexican Army to organize its first Escuadron de Caza by May 1, 1923. The pilots of this organization are seen here posed before the nose of the solitary Ansaldo A.1 Ballila, 1-D-79. (Tohtli via Santiago Flores).

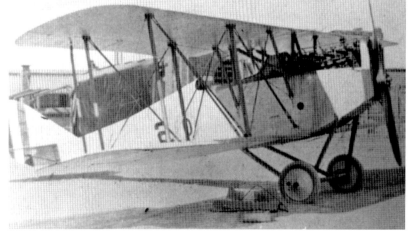

ABOVE: Along with the single-seat A.1 Ballila, Mexico also acquired one Ansaldo S.V.A.10 two-place combat aircraft, coded 2-D-80. (Tohtli via Santiago Flores)

RIGHT: The first purchase of state-of-the-art training aircraft by Mexico came in the form of ten Morane-Saulnier M.S.35E.P.-2s in August 1921, this one is coded 31-A-123. Some of these aircraft were armed and saw action during the revolutionary period. (via Ing. Jose Villela).

LEFT One of the first of the ten M.S.35E.P.-2s acquired in August 1921, 8-A-100 shows the manner in which Mexican aircraft were being marked at this juncture, with the large numeral '8' under the port wing and repeated on the upper right wing, inboard of the national insignia. The number '100' was carried in smaller numerals on the rudder. (via Hector Davila Cornejo).

BELOW: Seldom illustrated and sitting between a genuine Avro 504K on the right (13-A-105) and a De Havilland D.H.4B on the left, is one of the five or six Lincoln-Standard biplanes acquired by Mexico during the early 1920s. These aircraft apparently only carried simple serials, "1" to "5", outside the scheme then in use, although they did have standard national insignia and rudder stripes. (via Hector Davila Cornejo)

RIGHT: Although published and identified as a Curtiss JN-4D, this fully-marked Mexican service aircraft is in fact one of the similar, but little-known Brown Specials, coded 1-C-73. Note the equal span wings, shape of the elevators, and much longer vertical fin. (via Hector Davila Cornejo).

LEFT: One of a few known images of a genuine Mexican Army Curtiss JN-4D Jenny, with the name "Jalisco" emblazoned along the length of the fuselage with some unidentified art work on the rudder. The rear cockpit coaming appears to have been modified.
(via Ing. Jose Villela).

The ultimate expression of the much earlier T.N.C.A. Serie A came with the adoption of at least five of these aircraft with 230hp Salmson engines, including the first such conversion, 1-B-72, around November 1920, under the guidance of engineer Angel Lascurain. It is often cited as the Lascurain Salmson "A" type (note the distinctive rear fuselage and empennage).
(via Ing. Jose Villela)

ABOVE : Although Mexico purchased foreign aircraft after the shortcomings of her indigenous designs of 1917-1920 became evident, her engineers learned from the experience and produced designs such as the T.N.C.A./Lascurain Puro with a large Salmson radial engine imported from France. At least five were built, including 3-B-89 seen here. The rather unusual shape to the fin and rudder, are noteworthy, as is the synchronized forward firing fixed gun and rear gunner's circular cockpit . (via Ing. Jose Villela).

Finally with the end of the US embargo in January 1924, Mexico was quick to seek and acquire around 19 De Havilland D.H.4B reconnaissance bombers direct from U.S. Army stocks. Rushed to the scene of revolutionary skirmishes as soon as they arrived, they did not enjoy the luxury of contemporary Mexican markings, and were operated for some time in very crude condition.
(via Ing. Jose Villela)

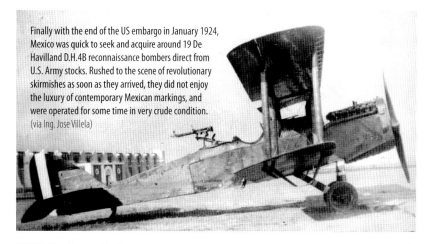

ABOVE: Eventually, the Mexican D.H.4Bs acquired national markings, rudder stripes and simple serials. Here, at Balbuena Field near Mexico City, parked before hangars "1" to "6", the first three named after martyrs of the air service, are serials "2" and "19".
(via Santiago Flores)

RIGHT: Seldom illustrated "in the field," this Mexican D.H.4B operating on the rough field near Irapuato in early 1924, shows no evidence of national markings or serials whatsoever.
(via Santiago Flores).

LEFT: Somewhat later on, D.H.4B serial number "10" had been refurbished and painted in full national markings - this photo in the field was probably taken circa 1926. (via Dr. Gary Kuhn).

ABOVE: Uniforms were rather non-standard "in the field" during the revolutionary period in Mexico! In the center, under this D.H.4Bs prop hub, is Coronel Ralph O'Neill, commander of the Mexican air forces during much of the early 1920s. He was credited with modernizing and effectively training the force. (via Manuel Ruiz Romero)

ABOVE: Apparently originally imported as a demonstrator, the Mexican air service acquired this solitary Hanriot, thought to have been an HD-19, circa 1925. It is believed to have been used as a trainer only.

(via Ing. Jose Villela)

ABOVE: The fourth phase of the seemingly never-ending turmoil in Mexico continued into 1926 and beyond. The Governor of the Distrito Norte de Baja California took the rather unusual step of ordering four new Douglas O-2C reconnaissance bombers in October, ostensibly for "state police work," though possibly as a hedge against further U.S. sanctions. Seldom illustrated, the aircraft eventually reached Mexico, where they were initially painted with large names on their fuselages, in addition to the standard Mexican national insignia. (via Ing. Jose Villela).

LEFT: Named "Pima" this is one of the four Baja California Douglas O-2Cs arriving rather ingloriously at the main Mexican Army shops at Balbuena. (via Hector Davila Cornejo).

ABOVE: A Boarhound II being started "the hard way". (via Santiago Flores)

LEFT: The Mexican purchasing commission sent to England also acquired two exotic Bristol Type 93B Boarhound IIs. They saw service during the Escobar revolution of 1928, assigned to each of the Commanders of the 1º and 2º Regimientos. Note that Bristol's also painted the national insignia incorrectly on the lower wings of these aircraft as well, as on the Bristol F.2Bs! (Cortes Foto via Santiago Flores)

ABOVE: Mexico once again turned to Europe for new combat types when the U.S. again introduced sanctions. A purchasing commission visited England and acquired at least 10 Bristol F.2B Fighters (c/n 7222 to 7231) in March 1928, sometimes known as the Mk.III/IV type. In their haste to take delivery, the manufacturer painted the national insignia on at least the lower wing panels in reverse! (via Dr. Gary Kuhn)

ABOVE: One T.N.C.A. Azcárate E-1, often incorrectly identified as the larger O-E-1, was fitted with twin Edo floats for possible naval applications. Serial "1" proved underpowered in service. (Herbert Photos)

ABOVE: With the type name on the vertical fin above the word Prototipo, the first T.N.A. Azcárate O-E-1 was used by FAM pilot Gustavo de Leon to make a number of long-distance, show-the-flag flights, touching down in every state in Mexico in 1928. Note the crests painted on the fuselage for the places visited. (via M.B. Passingham)

RIGHT: First flown in July 1928, the prototype T.N.A. Azcárate O-E-1 was a rather angular sesquiplane intended to fulfill Mexican combat aircraft requirements in the midst of the revolutionary period. The aircraft proved very difficult to control and most sources agree that only four were completed. (via Santiago Flores)

ABOVE: Juan F. Azcárate followed the largely unsuccessful O-E-1 with a scaled-down trainer version known as the E-1. Alleged to possess light handling and good combat potential, the aircraft was colloquially known as the "aviones blancos". Ten were built between September and December 1928 for the FAM. They featured a variety of engines, the last being Wright J-6s as shown here. (via Ing. Jose Villela)

ABOVE: The first of the Vought O2U-2 Corsairs acquired by Mexico on a rush basis in early 1929, sometimes cited as O2U-2Ms. This image has been printed this way several times before, and has led a number of observers to believe that the fixed-firing .30 caliber gun in the upper wing was on the port side. In fact, this image is reversed. Note the last three letters of the maker's name 'VOUGHT' in reverse on the fin. Additionally note the combination telescopic and ring-and-bead gun sight. Bomb racks and machine guns were installed at the factory by Vought. (United Technologies)

ABOVE: One of the 12 Vought O2U-2M Corsairs drawn hastily from the production line in early 1929, numbered '5' after completion of full FAM markings. Note the set of A-3 bomb racks under each lower ring and the Scarff ring in the rear cockpit. Additionally note the position of the fixed-firing .30 caliber. machine gun in the upper starboard wing panel. (David Ostrowski Collection)

ABOVE: Fine study of one of the 12 Vought-supplied O2U-2M Corsairs, showing the unique FAM serial number style in use during the Escobar revolutionary period of 1928-1929. (via Stephen Hudek Collection)

ABOVE: None other than General Plutarco Elias Calles (wearing flying helmet and goggles) and Coronel (P.A.) Pablo L. Sidar (adjusting the General's helmet) prepare for a flight in one of the Vought O2U-2M Corsairs to reconnoiter elements of the Escobar revolutionaries early in the fifth period of the Mexican Revolution. (via Santiago Flores).

Vought O2U-2M Corsair, '11', Fuerza Aérea Mexicana, Mexico, Escobar revolutionary period, 1928-29

LEFT, BELOW LEFT: Two views of four of the Waco Model 10-T/220 Taperwings acquired hastily by the Mexican Government early in the Escobar Revolt. Note that all four bear completely different color schemes. Their 'armament' in the field reportedly consisted of Thompson .45 caliber sub machine guns, hand-held by the observer, and bags of hand grenades! (via Charles N. Trask)

ABOVE: One of the few U.S. manufacturers that was able to respond with almost immediate delivery on semi-prepared "combat" aircraft at the height of the Escobar Revolt was Waco. These four Model 10-Ts, also cited in some Waco documents as "220 Taperwings" were nearly identical to those sold to Brazil. Their armament is unknown and, to date, not a single example of one in full FAM markings has surfaced. At delivery, each of the aircraft had a completely different civil color scheme! (Aero Digest)

BELOW: One of the more elegant aircraft to serve the Mexican Government during the Escobar revolt, the Cessna CW-5, named Magdita in FAM service, eventually received the registration X-BACX. It was essentially commandeered on March 11th.
(Bob Pickett Collection)

RIGHT: Frequently misidentified as one of the Stinson SM-1B Detroiters expropriated by the Government and used during the 1929 Escobar Revolt. This aircraft was in fact a Travel Air Model 6000, formerly U.S. civil registration C-8013 (msn 814). The 1929 campaigns were marked by the use of an extraordinary variety of aircraft that happened upon the scene.
(via Ing. Jose Villela)

ABOVE: Virtually any aircraft the Mexican Government could lay its hands on became a 'military' type. Here, certainly one of the few - if not the only example of a Buhl CA-6 Airsedan, bears full FAM insignia, but no serial, during the 1929 emergency.
(via Hector Davila Cornejo)

LEFT: In this view at a remote operating base at Uruapan, Michoacan, one of seven Stinson SM-1Bs impressed into FAM service from the S.C.O.P. fleet early in the revolution of 1928-1929. The outer lower wing panels appear to have been painted a bright color, with the national insignia over laid on top.

RIGHT: Following on the generally favorable impression made by a batch of Douglas O-2Cs acquired earlier, Mexico placed a substantial order, spurred by the Escobar Revolt, for 15 updated variants known as O-2Ms and O-2M-2s with 525hp Pratt & Whitney engines. Serial 13 later gained prominence while used as a mount for a number of long-distance flights.
(via Stephen Hudek Collection)

BELOW: Yet another exotic aircraft to enter service with the Escobar rebels was a Waterhouse Cruzair, msn 1, formerly U.S. Identified Aircraft #1724. It entered Mexico sometime after March 24, 1929. The design has obvious Ryan/Mahoney influences.
(P. & A. Photo)

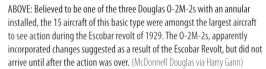

ABOVE: Believed to be one of the three Douglas O-2M-2s with an annular installed, the 15 aircraft of this basic type were amongst the largest aircraft to see action during the Escobar revolt of 1929. The O-2M-2s, apparently incorporated changes suggested as a result of the Escobar Revolt, but did not arrive until after the action was over. (McDonnell Douglas via Harry Gann)

LEFT: The Escobarista rebels operated a number of diverse aircraft during the revolt as well, including this Curtiss OX-5 powered American Eagle A-1, formerly U.S. civil C-7490 (msn 302), with the distinctive American Eagle logo still emblazoned on the rudder!
(Hagedorn Collection)

LEFT: Very rare 1929 photo of the Escobar American Eagle A-1 and a Thunderbird W-14 on railroad flat cars just before crossing from Mexico into El Paso for repairs.
(Library of Congress)

ABOVE: Pleased with the performance turned out by the Vought O2U-2M Corsairs during the 1929 Escobar Rebellion, the Mexican Government arranged to license-build the type in Mexico with the Fábrica Juan F. Azcárate. After considerable trials and tribulations, the first such aircraft, appropriately named "5 de Mayo" serial "1" was delivered in May 1931. (Ing. Enrique Velasco via Santiago Flores)

ABOVE: Subsequent follow-on batches of Azcárate Corsarios followed for the FAM, and serial number "32" is shown with special red chevrons on the upper main plane, and broad bands flowing aft from the gunners cockpit. (Ing. Enrique Velasco via Santiago Flores)

ABOVE: For reasons that are not clear, many documents identify the bulk of the Mexican license-built Corsarios by a U.S. Navy designation - O2U-4A. They were structurally very similar. Serial number "40" shown here continues to display the characteristic FAM numeral style of the 1930s. (via Stephen Hudek)

Azcárate O2U-2M Corsario, '32', Fuerza Aérea Mexicana, Escobar Rebellion, 1929

Azcárate O2U-2M Corsario, 5 de Mayo, serial '1', Mexico, May 1931

ABOVE: Believed to be a post-May 1931 lineup of nine of the first 10 Azcárate-built Corsarios, the nearest aircraft, serial number "2" appears to have two fixed-firing .30 caliber gun mounts in the mid-upper wing, the port gun barrel showing prominently. Essentially similar to the O2U-2Ms acquired from Vought, a number of modifications were incorporated later. (via Santiago Flores)

ABOVE: The O2U-2Ms and Mexican-built Corsarios gave excellent service and were almost an ideal aircraft for the Mexican operating conditions. Serial number "52" sits next to a Lend-Lease North American AT-6B in a hangar at Balbuena in 1942. (via Ing. Enrique Velasco via Santiago Flores)

ABOVE: Azcárate-built Corsarios were easily identifiable by two means. First, the distinctive logo of the builder on the vertical fin and the individual aircraft serials. Anything above number "12" was Mexican-built. Some aircraft were fitted with Townend Rings in Mexico in an effort to improve performance and cooling. Serial number "60" has a windscreen for the gunner of the type often seen on U.S. Navy O2U-4s. (via Ing. Jose Villela)

ABOVE: Oddly, the exact number of Corsarios built under license in Mexico is open to debate. Serials reached at least "65," but this series is muddied by the introduction of much later Vought V.99Ms in the midst of the licence production. Serial number "63" bears fuselage bands of an unknown color, much farther aft than on other similar examples. (Ing. Enrique Velasco via Santiago Flores)

ABOVE: Never illustrated before, at least one Corsario was fitted with a canopy, possibly appropriated from Mexico's single Stearman Model 81. (via Dr. Miguel Narro)

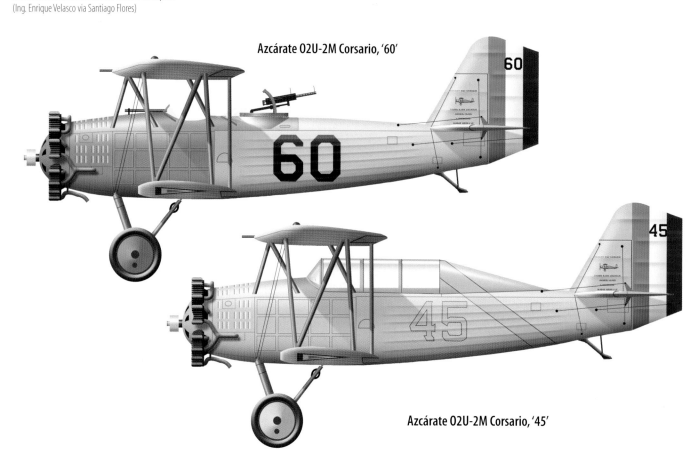

Azcárate O2U-2M Corsario, '60'

Azcárate O2U-2M Corsario, '45'

LEFT: The delays in delivery of the Mexican license-built Vought O2U-4As led the FAM to acquire a number of exotic aircraft in the early 1930s for evaluation in the event that Azcárate was unable to complete the job. One was a Stearman Model 81, complete with a canopy cover over the two crew positions. It was apparently capable of carrying armament, but the exact arrangement remains unclear. (via Ing. Jose Villela).

LEFT: Often mis-identified as Kreider-Reisner, the FAM also acquired at least two rare Royal Bird B trainers in April 1930 with Kinner K-5 engines. This example appears to have the insignia of the EAM on the fuselage, but no serial. In many FAM strength reports, they were listed only as "Royals". (via Ing. Jose Villela)

ABOVE: The successor to the Azcárate E-1 sesquiplane trainers, but judged by most Mexican pilots as not being as good, were seven Kreider-Reisner KR-34Cs. Acquired in early June 1930, coded 1E to 7E, they were intended as multi-purpose aircraft. The Wright J-6-5 powered trainers were to total nearly 70 aircraft, but this did not eventuate.

RIGHT: Another multi-purpose aircraft acquired between November 1931 and 1933 were at least 12 Spartan C-3-120s. There is some evidence that some may have seen action as light reconnaissance-bombers. (Ing. Jose Villela).

This exceptionally rare photograph of an FAM Spartan C-3-120, C-4-A, can be dated from the other rare aircraft in the background - the hulk of XA-BDG, a Stinson Model U minus all three engines, the first new examples of which did not appear until 1932. The Spartan, acquired in 1933, is unusual in having a Donald Duck caricature deploying a parachute on the fuselage. (via Dave Ostrowski)

ABOVE: Evolution of FAM training and support aircraft in the closing years of the revolutionary period continued with the acquisition of six Fleet (Canada) F-10-32Ds in September 1936 coded E-1 to E-6. These aircraft have been frequently mis-identified. (via Francis "Diz" Dean)

ABOVE: The final, pre-Lend-Lease training aircraft acquired by the FAM, and the first modern monoplanes, were six Ryan STA Specials delivered in January 1938. Often quoted in error as STMs, they were coded "1" to "6" but did not have armament capability. (via Santiago Flores)

ABOVE: Acquired for the Comisión Nacional de Irigación in 1936 as CNI-1, a single Fairchild (Canada) Model 82B, msn 45, was apparently impressed into FAM service for duty during the final phase of revolutionary activity, the Cedillista Rebellion. (via Sam Parker)

BELOW: Certainly the most modern aircraft operated on behalf of the FAM during the final phase of the revolution was a single Lockheed 12-A, msn 1239, delivered in January 1938. It was marked as XB-ABW and named Presidente Carranza. (via William Haines)

LEFT: The penultimate combat aircraft type acquired during the last phase of the Mexican Revolution were 10 Consolidated Model 21-M multi-purpose aircraft, coded 22 to 31. These replaced the ancient Bristol F.2Bs of the 3º Escuadron of the 1º Regimiento by January 1937, but proved most disappointing in service. Note the rear gun, flare chutes on the lower fuselage and the engine cowl on serial number "31" the last example. (via Santiago Flores)

ABOVE: One of the first things to go on the Consolidated Model 21-Ms in service were the tight-fitting engine cowls, as the engines tended to overheat in the field. Note the A-3 bomb racks under the lower wing. (via Ing. Jose Villela)

RIGHT: The last Vought Corsair biplane production line models were V-99-Ms for Mexico, one of the first poses at the factory in December 1937. These were the primary combat mounts of the FAM during the Cedillo Rebellion. (Vought).

ABOVE: Lineup of all 10 Mexican Vought V-99-Ms just before their delivery flight. For reasons unknown, the aircraft received serial numbers drawn from amongst those assigned to Mexican-built O2U-4As. They had A-3 bomb racks under each lower wing. (Vought)

ABOVE: Taken in the field during the Cedillo Rebellion, these are almost certainly the five aircraft that saw action. Visible are serial numbers 44 (nearest), 32 34 and 35, with two-color bands around the rear fuselage of each aircraft. (via Ing. Jose Villela)

Vought V-99-M Corsair, '44', Cedillo Rebellion

ABOVE: Photographs of the rather cosmopolitan assortment of aircraft acquired and operated on behalf of the insurgent Cedillo are exceptionally rare, but this Howard DGA-8, subsequently incorporated into the FAM as serial "69" was either msn 82 or 83. These had been spirited into Mexico in September 1937 and served as light bombers in Cedillo service. (via Santiago Flores)

RIGHT: The FAM mixed unit that operated in the field against Cedillo is known to have been supported by a Stinson aircraft known only by its quasi-civil registration, XB-ABB. It is believed to have been this hybrid aircraft, which had unusual paint on the lower wing panels and an unidentified crest on the starboard door. (via Stephen Hudek)

Vought V-99-M Corsair, '38', San Luis Potosi, Cedillo Rebellion

ABOVE: At least two of the Vought V-99-Ms operated in San Luis Potosi against Cedillo are known to have received crude camouflage while in the field, including serial number "38" seen here. The colors, unfortunately, are unknown, but were probably acquired locally - and may in fact have been made from local soil! (Casasala via Santiago Flores)

ABOVE: Vought V-99-M serial number "39" apparently suffered damage during the Cedillo operations with the Escuadrón Aéreo Mixto, but was able to return to base. (via Santiago Flores)

LEFT: Another of the V-99-Ms which received crude field camouflage, apparently including the undersides of the wings, served as a backdrop for the flight personnel of the Escuadrón Aéreo Mixto that flew against Cedillo in 1938 in San Luis Potosi. (Library of Congress).

2 Unrest in Brazil — The Camphana do Contestado / Aviação da Brigada Militar - Rio Grande do Sul

1914 1915

While monumental political and military events were evolving far to the north in Mexico and in Europe, by September 1914, political forces were also at work in remote regions of Brazil, Latin America's largest nation.

Years earlier, in 1835, the Brazilian province of Paraná had been created from territory carved from the traditional and existing São Paulo province, but with very poorly defined borders. During the ensuing decades, local disputes over the definitions of these boundaries, and questions even of loyalty and allegiance to the Brazilian monarchy, ebbed and surged through the area.

By September 1914, the social and economic forces fueling these continuing clashes had come to be cited as the *Campanha do Contestado* and the Brazilian Federal Army finally found it expedient to employ the new science of aeronautics to aid ground forces in quelling the regional insurrectionists. Two Brazilian Army airmen, together with five aircraft – four Morane-Saulniers of various types and the inevitable Blériot XI –

made history by becoming the first aviators in mainland South America to operate aircraft in a combat environment. More details describing the exploits of these airmen, which commenced in 1914, can be found in the downloadable main text.

Later, in August 1915, close on the heels of the troubles in São Paulo, the Brazilian state of Rio Grande do Sul created an aviation unit which was planned to support the state para-military force, known as the *Aviação Brigadiana*. The idea languished, mainly due to the continuing World War and the concurrent difficulty in obtaining equipment.It was not formally activated, as the *Serviço de Aviação da Brigada* until May 1923, equipped with two war-surplus Breguet Bre 14s acquired in Argentina. With these, the organization carried out a number of missions in connection with the state para-military force to contain various small bandit and rebel groups. Although short-lived, this force represented the first use of aircraft in Latin America as weapons in support of police activities at less than the national level.

3 Brazil - The Copacabana Revolt

1922

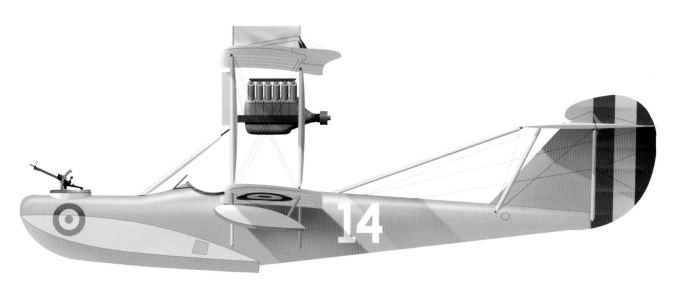

Curtiss HS-2L, '14', Escola de Aviação Naval, Brazil, July 1922

While individual states and provinces within Brazil had found it expedient to form their own internal military aviation units, the central Government moved more slowly, only creating the forbear to the present day Brazilian Air Force (*Força Aérea Brasileira*) in November 1918, as the *Serviço de Aviação Militar*.

However, the Brazilian Navy had formed an aviation element ahead of the Army – the *Escola de Aviação Naval* in August 1916.

It was Curtiss HS-2L flying boats of the Naval service that became not only the first Brazilian national aircraft to see action in Latin America, but the first strictly Naval aircraft to do so. Although only a very brief affair, the one-day revolt by young officers at the *Forte de Copacabana*, in sympathy with political elements in Brazilian society, was overawed by the bombardment of the fort and surrounding area by at least two Navy HS-2Ls on July 5, 1922.

4 Brazil - Tenente's Revolt

1924 1927

Breguet Bre 14, Escola de Aviação Militar, Brazil, 1924
French aircraft predominated in early Brazilian Army aviation, and one of the most important types was the ubiquitous Bréguet Bre 14. This example, named Ánhangá (a Tupy-Guarany word meaning "devil"), a Bre 14A2, is typically painted for the period of internal turmoil in Brazil that lasted from 1924-1927.

The abortive Copacabana revolt of 1922, outlined in Chapter Three, was only the beginning of a period of internal discord within Brazil, and especially within the ranks of the junior officer corps of the Army and its infant air service.

Centered in São Paulo, the loyal elements of the Brazilian Army were reinforced by officers and NCO pilots drawn mainly from the *Escola de Aviação Militar* (EAM) and in mid-July 1924, using an assortment of French aircraft including Breguet 14A-2 reconnaissance bombers, Nieuport 24bisE-1 and SPAD-Herbemont S.54Ep-2 trainers, at least 21 bombing missions were carried out against rebel elements.

The Brazilian Navy aviation organization also took part in operations against the rebels, mounting a number of reconnaissance missions using a pair of Curtiss F-5L flying boats, two smaller Curtiss HS-2Ls and two old Curtiss MFs. Their primary contribution was to isolate the rebels from reinforcement from surface vessels.

The rebels themselves are also known to have employed commandeered aircraft, including at least two Curtiss Orioles, although these were used for reconnaissance and leaflet missions for the most part,

but on one mission, home-made bombs were carried as well. Hoping for a bold stroke, two rebel airmen even flew one of the Orioles to Rio, with a view towards bombing the official residence of the President of the Republic, which was successful, if not inflicting much damage.

Loyal forces bombarded the main rebel positions and forced them to take to the interior, where a combination of Army and Navy aircraft continued to pursue them well into March 1925.

Rebel elements, in the meantime, reconstituted themselves, and somehow managed to acquire Curtiss JN-4Ds and a locally modified Huff-Daland H.D.5 Petrel, known as the *Anhangüera*, but never ending problems of logistics, spares, and fuel supply limited their usefulness.

The continuing campaign against the rebels exhausted the Army aviation element, when it was in its infancy. By the end, only two aircraft were actually airworthy and capable of operations. The campaign was, in effect, however, a right of passage for the service, and in January 1927, it was reorganized and rejuvenated. The main text download discusses this transformation in detail.

5 Paraguayan Revolution

1922

The Paraguayan Revolution of 1922 was the culmination of a seemingly never ending series of factional feuds that had been continuing in the virtually land-locked nation since 1904.

A less likely venue for the employment of aircraft – by both sides, including classic air-to-air combat for the first time in Latin America – would be difficult to imagine. Paraguay had enjoyed only very brief exposure to aeronautics, but powerful factions with adequate funds had not missed the lessons of the Great War, and realized that aircraft might provide the edge that would lead their cause to victory.

The introduction of aircraft by both the sitting Ayala Government and rebel elements was apparently premeditated, and no doubt facilitated by the ready availability of fairly capable aircraft and under-employed airmen from several nations, in nearby Argentina.

Ironically, one of the first aircraft to reach Government factions

was none other than a First World War vintage Armstrong Whitworth F.K.8, so far as can be ascertained, the only aircraft of this series to ever operated in Latin America. Flown in during June 1922, the Government decided to reinforce this aircraft with at least six more aircraft, all of Great War Italian vintage.

Within weeks, impressed by the Government use of aircraft to some effect, the rebel elements likewise recruited veterans of the war from Argentina and, by July, were also flying former Italian aircraft.

The main text describes, for the first time, the operational use of this amazing collection of aircraft, plus others, and the exertions that their crews endured to make them effective against the opposition. Sporadic aerial engagements and attack missions continued on and off as late as May 1923.

Ansaldo SVA-10, '1', Ñu-Guazú (Campo Grande),
Paraguayan Revolution, 1922

LEFT: One of the first aircraft to reach Paraguay for use in the revolution was an obscure First World War Armstrong-Whitworth F.K.8. Seen here being prepared for transport to the base near Asuncion, it had already been emblazoned with the name "Pres. Ayala" on its fuselage. (Museo de Historia Militar via Antonio Luis Sapienza)

ABOVE: Another view of the only Armstrong-Whitworth F.K.8 to reach Latin America, being unloaded from a river boat at Asuncion. The rudder had been painted white, possibly to obscure its former RFC markings. It apparently had the name "Pres. Ayala" painted on the starboard fuselage side only. (Museo de Historia Militar via Antonio Luis Sapienza).

ABOVE:At least two Italian-built S.A.M.L. A.3 (sometimes given as S.1s) biplanes were acquired in Argentina for use by the Gubernista forces in the early days of the Paraguayan Revolution of 1922.
(Archivo Cap. Nav. J. R. Ocampos via Antonio Luis Sapienza)

ABOVE: Apparently at least one Gubernista Ansaldo SVA-5 and a SVA-10 were armed with a single .45-caliber Thompson sub-machine gun braced to fire forward on the upper wing, as shown here. The rear gunner has been additionally provided with a hand-held version. The crew consists of Sgto. Nicola Bó and Sgto. Francisco Cusmanich. Note also the crude bombs suspended by rope from the rear cockpit.
(Antonio Luis Sapienza Collection)

LEFT: Former RFC pilot Lt. Patrick Hassett, a Great War veteran, flew for the Gubernistas during the 1922 revolution, and is seen here in front of an Ansaldo SVA-5 fighter.
(Museu de Historia Militar via Antonio Luis Sapienza)

ABOVE: Both Ansaldo SVA-5s and SVA-10s saw extensive use during the 1922 Paraguayan Revolution. Here, an SVA-10 is introduced to loyalist troops at the airfield at Ñu-Guazú (Campo Grande) during the height of the action.
(Museo de Historia Militar via Antonio Luis Sapienza)

LEFT: In 1923, the Gubernista air arm that had served so well during the 1922 revolution was formalized with the creation of the Escuela de Aviación Militar (EMA) at Ñu-Guazú aerodrome. The initial equipment included aircraft left over at the end of the fighting, both Government-owned and those seized from the rebels. From left to right is one of the Ansaldo SVA-10 (coded "1" in the white portion of the horizontal rudder stripes), an SVA-5 (coded "2") and the fuselage of an S.A.M.L. A.3 (S.1) (Antonio Luis Sapienza Collection)

BELOW: In May 1927, the Paraguayan EMA received one Morane-Saulnier M.S.139E.p.-2 and three Hanriot H.D.-32E.p.-2 trainers. These joined one of the sole survivors of the 1922 revolution, a single S.A.M.L. A.3 (S.1), in this classic line-up shortly after arrival. (via George von Roitberg)

6 Chilean Military Intervention  1925 1932

Curtiss D-12 Falcon, '3', Fuerza Aérea Nacional, Chile, 1931-32

In January 1925, the Chilean military establishment intervened in the political life of the nation as a result of a combination of economic distress, political stalemate and to facilitate change in the existing political system. However, an underlying motivation was a general sense that the ruling establishment had allowed the military to stagnate following the turn of the century, and many Chilean officers felt that national prestige, which had always sought to maintain par with the other Latin American power-houses (Brazil, Argentina and Peru) was in jeopardy.

The result, by 1927, was a first in Latin American military history, and witnessed most of the Chilean Army and its emerging air arm (the *Fuerza Aérea Nacional*, or FAN), pitted against the Chilean Navy, each service having adopted opposing views on the events as they unfolded.

In some instances, Army and Navy units located near one another had adopted similar stances, leading to a very confused state of affairs.

To this volatile mix must be added several personalities who had reached influential levels on the Chilean political stage, not least of which was Marmaduke Grove, *Director General de Aeronáutica* as of 1925. Indeed, by 1931-32, Grove had risen from Major to Commodore and to the leadership of a so-called Socialist Republic, and his imprint on the evolution of Chilean aviation during the same period was profound. From the mix of some 100 British aircraft of World War vintage, the national air arm had transitioned to a mix of Curtiss P-1A and P-1B Hawk fighters, Curtiss D-12 Falcon attack and reconnaissance-bombers, Vickers Vixen V bombers, Vickers-Wibault Type 121 Scouts and, not least, nine Junkers R.42 heavy bombers, the most modern bomber force in all of Latin America. A host of other aircraft, including Dornier Wal reconnaissance-bomber flying boats for the Naval cooperation units, rounded out a vastly improved aviation force.

Unfortunately, while huge strides had been taken in expanding and modernizing the armed forces, in particular the aviation elements, there had been little in the way of training to prepare crews to operate these newer machines. In the midst of all of this, personnel and units of the FAN had been engaged in a seemingly endless series of intrigues and shifting allegiances, which no doubt impacted their readiness.

Matters reached boiling point in 1931 when *General* Enrique Bravo ascended to power, triggering much more intense confrontations throughout the nation, and a nearly complete mutiny within the Navy of junior officers, petty officers and sailors against their ranking officers. In September, the Government instructed the leadership of the FAN

to move against the commandeered fleet and, as a direct result, for the first time, a coordinated attack against major surface vessels was organized by aircraft, consisting of nine Curtiss D-12 Falcons, two of the Junkers R.42s and, to the astonishment of many, one of the Ford 5-AT-C Trimotors operated by the quasi-military airline LAN, which was engaged as an ad hoc heavy bomber.

Although the attack resulted in few casualties, it proved sobering in the extreme to the Naval personnel who were on the receiving end, and especially so when they were advised that, if they did not surrender forthwith, another attack involving not less then 40 aircraft would be mounted the following day!

See the on-line download text on the publisher's website for further details of this fascinating and little-known episode.

LEFT: One of the first truly modern aircraft acquired for evaluation by Chile was a single Junkers A 20 two-seat tactical aircraft. Marked J 7, it was received in early December 1924, on the eve of the internal strife and served throughout the intervention period. (via Lennart Andersson)

ABOVE: To modernize her training element at the beginning of the intervention period, the Chilean Army acquired 12 obscure Bristol Model P.T.M. Lucifer multi-purpose aircraft, most of which had been delivered by July 1926. Here, two of the P.T.M.s seem to have had a rather unfortunate introduction to a Junkers R 42 bomber. (via Günther Ott)

RIGHT: Two of the first nine rather ungainly Vickers Type 116 Vixen V reconnaissance bombers, which began to arrive in Chile around January 1926. (Fuerza Aérea de Chile)

ABOVE: Although billed at the time as one of the most advanced, all-metal pursuit types in the world, the 26 Vickers-Wibault Type 121 Scouts acquired by the Chilean Army in 1927 were difficult to land, as evidenced by an all-too-common problem shown here by No.3. (Fuerza Aérea de Chile)

ABOVE: Some Chilean pilots said that, upon landing, if the heavy metal wings started to tip from side-to-side during the roll-out, a nose-over or ground loop was inevitable. The aircraft also suffered from lack of rudder authority at low speeds, which exacerbated the landing problem. (Fuerza Aérea de Chile)

Vickers-Wibault Type 121 Scout, 10, Fuerza Aérea Nacional, Chile, 1927

LEFT: Although a sturdy aircraft and able to handle rough fields, this Chilean Curtiss D-12 Falcon, No.9, came to grief at the hands of a pilot new to the type. It was repaired, and continued on in service as late as January 1938. (Fuerza Aerea de Chile)

ABOVE: Chile acquired a large number of De Havilland D.H. 60 Moth variants, commencing with Cirrus Moths. Note that this example (to the left), operating for the military airmail line LAN, features tri-color rudder stripes, while the Junkers R 42, J3, in the background bears the all-blue rudder with a white star superimposed, and the national insignia on the fuselage in use at the time. (Fuerza Aérea de Chile)

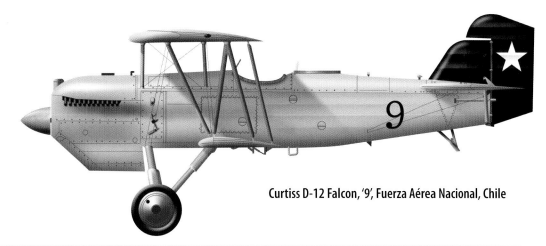

Curtiss D-12 Falcon, '9', Fuerza Aérea Nacional, Chile

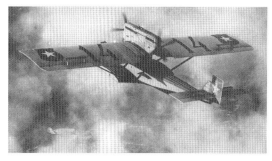

TOP/ABOVE: Two views of one of the first Rolls-Royce Eagle IX-powered Dornier Wal flying boats acquired in Italy for the Chilean Navy in 1926.
(Heinz J. Nowarra and Fuerza Aérea de Chile)

ABOVE: Besides the Curtiss D-12-powered Hawks, Chile also acquired a fleet of Curtiss Falcons as well. No.3 displays full period markings
(Fuerza Aérea de Chile)

RIGHT: Curtiss Falcons were amongst the aircraft that saw action against rebellious Chilean Naval vessels during the intervention period, including No.4 shown here.
(Fuerza Aérea de Chile)

ABOVE: Chile acquired six Canadian-built Vickers Vedette Vs in 1929, No.2 being shown here on 13 December after an exploration flight by Cdte. Arturo Merino Benitez, in company with a Loening/Keystone Air Yacht to Río Palena.
(Colección MUNACH No.3589)

LEFT: The Naval component of the Fuerza Aérea Nacional acquired two variants of the Fairey IIIF, some of which were routinely catapulted from Chilean Navy capital ships, such as No.3 shown here.
(Author's Collection)

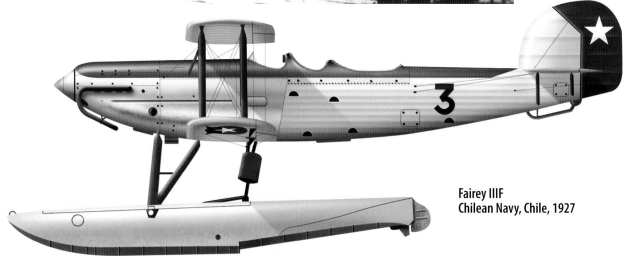

Fairey IIIF
Chilean Navy, Chile, 1927

LEFT: The Chilean battle cruiser Almirante Latorre, which figured prominently as a pawn - and a target - during the Naval rebellion.
(Fuerza Aérea de Chile)

ABOVE/RIGHT: Chile also acquired examples of the durable Ford Tri-Motor for use by its internal airline, LAN, at least one of which was outfitted as a bomber during the intervention.

Nicaraguan Revolution

1927

The so-called "era of interventions" that persisted in Central America and the Caribbean region between 1909 and 1933 witnessed a gradual awakening to the utility of aircraft as a means of exerting influence on the course of events.

Although usually modest, and making use of conventional aircraft with mercenary crews as make-shift bombers and light attack aircraft, the sporadic incidents are noteworthy. In at least one instance, that of itinerant airman Lowell Yerex in Honduras, the sitting caudillo who benefited from the intervention of several lightly armed aircraft was so grateful that he financed the nascent TACA airline as a direct result, an international airline that flourished and exists to this day.

In impoverished Nicaragua, the so-called "Second Intervention" of 1925-26 by U.S. Marines resulted in the establishment of the first truly indigenous national military force, the *Guardia Nacional*, which soon degenerated into little more than an instrument of the ruling clique, and which eventually led to the alienation of the average citizenry.

Through a series of internal political moves, the sitting Chamorro regime in power as of August 1926 experienced increasing opposition, which escalated into armed conflict. The emergence of the legendary rebel leader Augusto César Sandino by mid-1927 led almost directly to the introduction of both U.S. Marine Corps aircraft and Nicaraguan Government aircraft into the equation.

The Chamorro Government, known as the Conservatives, hired two U.S. mercenaries and purchased three Swallow aircraft (followed by a fourth later) in the U.S. which, although hardly military aircraft, were immediately available at a reasonable price. The two pilots then set about adapting their rather tired mounts to the task at hand, using locally-made pipe bombs, hand-held pistols and rifles as offensive armament.

Although little-known and of limited effectiveness, this episode witnessed the birth of the Nicaraguan Air Force and the principles of close-support developed by U.S. Marine aviators during the campaigns there. The on-line download text expands on these in detail.

LEFT: Turned out in full uniform, Mayors Lee Mason, sitting, and Bill Brooks pose beside one of the Laird Swallow biplanes that were pressed into the service of the Nicaraguan Government against insurgent forces in 1927. (Author's Collection)

The Chaco War - Paraguay and Bolivia

1928 1935

Curtiss Cyclone Falcon, Fuerza Aérea Boliviana, Villa Montes, Bolivia, 1924-27

The aviation aspects of the Chaco War have often been minimized or even ignored completely by historians of this, the first conventional war using modern weapons between two nation states in Latin America in the 20th Century.

While it is true that the numbers of aircraft engaged by both of the belligerents was never large, it is equally true that both made repeated and concerted efforts to expand their aviation elements throughout the period, but were stymied in doing so by a combination of embargoes by supplier nations, shipping challenges owing to the distances and land-locked nature of the combatants, and training of crews to man any aircraft acquired.

Bolivia clearly hoped to capitalize on the use of the airplane as a weapon, and invested heavily in equipping her service with the best aircraft available, which were to have eventually included Curtiss-Wright Condor strategic bombers. Paraguay, for her part, fought the war with essentially the same aircraft she had at the outset, with but few additions during the course of the conflict. Interestingly, it turned out to be a contest between the best of U.S. and European built and

designed equipment, since although Bolivia started the war with British and French built warplanes, she ended it with a force equipped almost entirely with state-of-the-art Curtiss and Curtiss-Wright aircraft, mixed with a few European Junkers aircraft of great capabilities but limited numbers. Paraguay, on the other hand, operated French and Italian equipment almost exclusively, but only a smattering of U.S. and British types.

The downloadable main text, taken together with the exhaustive book on the subject by this writer and Antonio Sapienza (Schiffer Publishing Ltd, 1997), brings fresh information on this poorly documented subject to the fore, including a number of first-hand observations made by military attachés who witnessed the events that have not been published elsewhere.

Additionally, the main text explores some of the combat claims made by the opposing forces, and analyses them in depth. The introduction of additional aircraft into the conflict is also discussed, as well as a number of mysterious reports that allude to aircraft that cannot otherwise be accounted for during the conflict.

LEFT: Starting in April 1927, Paraguay had to practically reinvent her infant air arm. Here, one of two Morane-Saulnier M.S.35E.p.-2s bearing full Paraguayan national markings. These nimble trainers prepared many Paraguayan pilots for what was to follow. (Collection Anibal Ferreira via Antonio Luis Sapienza).

ABOVE: Nearly the entire Bolivian Cuerpo de Aviadores at El Alto near La Paz on September 14, 1929. Nearest is Junkers W34 Vanguardia, with three named and aluminum-doped Breguet Bre 19A2s and three Caudron C.97 multi-purpose aircraft. (Ramiro Molina Alanes)

LEFT: The first aerial action of what was to become the Chaco War involved an attack by Bolivian Breguet Bre 19s and Fokker CVbs on Paraguayan military installations at Bahía Negra in December 1928. Here, Bolivian Bre 19A2 Batallon Colorados, believed to have been one of the aircraft involved in the attack, is christened in a ceremony at La Paz. (Ramiro Molina Alanes)

Breguet Bre 19, Fuerza Aérea Boliviana, La Paz, Bolivia, 1928

ABOVE: The second Paraguayan Potez 25A-2, with its distinctive numerals showing clearly, in this picture from 1929. This was the first Paraguayan Potez 25 lost, to an accident, that year. Note the twin guns hanging over the starboard side, with their stocks clearly evident.
(Tte. Emilio Rocholl via Antonio Luis Sapienza)

ABOVE: One of the earliest known photographs of one of the first ten Potez 25A-2 reconnaissance bombers delivered, taken shortly after assembly at the Ñu-Guazú aerodrome in 1928. Note the auxiliary fuel tank under the upper starboard wing and extended radiator. (Cnel. Av. A. Pasmor via Antonio Luis Sapienza)

LEFT: A proud maintenance crew stands before the first Paraguayan Potez 25A-2, serial number '1' in the hangar at Ñu-Guazú aerodrome in 1929. The rudder of No.2, with its French-style lettering, is just visible on the right. (Museo de Historia Militar via Antonio Luis Sapienza)

ABOVE: The Fokker CVbs acquired by Bolivia saw only limited service during the ensuing conflict, although one of these carried out one of the first aerial attacks of the war, in company with a Breguet Bre 19A2. (Ramiro Molina Alanes)

LEFT: The Paraguayan training establishment was augmented in 1927 with one Morane-Saulnier M.S.139E.p.-2, coded E.5. Here posing for the camera are, Tte. Leandro Aponte in the front cockpit, and Tte.2º Emilio Rocholl in the rear. Emilio Rocholl was the first Paraguayan pilot to be killed in combat during the war,. (via Antonio Luis Sapienza)

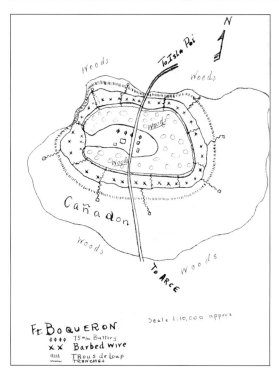

ABOVE: The solitary M.S.139 was characterized by a slightly swept wing. Along with the M.S.35 and Hanriot H.D.32s, these aircraft honed the skills of nearly all the wartime Paraguayan combat pilots. This 1932 photo shows that the M.S.139 had not as yet gained its ultimate serial number, E.5. (Museo de Historia Militar via Antonio Luis Sapienza)

ABOVE: A map of the almost legendary Fortín Boquerón and its environs.

RIGHT: A group of young Paraguayan pilots pose with the single M.S.139E.p.-2 at Ñu-Guazú, by this time displaying its serial number, E.5. The nature of the small insignia on the engine cowling is unknown. (via Antonio Luis Sapienza)

ABOVE: Virtually the entire component of the Paraguayan Arma Aérea, Escuela de Aviación Militar (EAM), at Ñu-Guazú aerodrome in 1929. From right to left, the aircraft are a single Breda Ba 15 (still bearing Italian registration I-AAUG), the M.S.139E.p.-2, the M.S.35E.p.-2, a Hanriot H.D.32E.p.-2, three Potez 25s and five Wibault Type 73C.1s. (via Antonio Luis Sapienza)

ABOVE: This view of one of the Paraguayan Wibault 73C.1 fighters at Isla Poí operating base reveals that, besides the national insignia in all four wing positions, the individual serial was also carried on both upper and lower surfaces of the wing. (Ministerio de Defensa Nacional via Antonio Luis Sapienza)

LEFT: Tte. Jose Gregorio Morinigo poses before his Wibault 73C.1, serial '5' at the rugged forward operating base at Isla Poí in August 1932. (Cnel.Av. Agustin Pasmor via Antonio Luis Sapienza)

ABOVE: Paraguayan crews pose before one of the few remaining Wibault 73C-1 at a deployment location in the Chaco. For Reasons unkown, No.23 was serialed out-of-sequence with the earlier aircraft.
(Leigh Wade Collection, USAF Archives)

Wibault 73C-1, '23', Paraguayan Arma Aérea, Chaco, ca 1929

ABOVE: The large oval radiator and painted chin cowl, reveals this otherwise unidentified Paraguayan Potez as a 25A.2 at Isla Poí in 1932. Note the distinctive underwing auxiliary fuel tank. (Cnel.Av. Agustin Pasmor via Antonio Luis Sapienza).

ABOVE: Tte. Agustin Pasmor, then chief of maintenance for the Paraguayan Arma Aérea, and one of the great unsung heroes of the conflict, poses in his flying togs beside a Potez 25T.O.E. at Concepción while enroute to the forward base at Isla Poí in 1932. The lower cowling of the T.O.E.s, unlike the 25A.2s, was kept free of paint to ease maintenance of oil leaks, the remainder of the aircraft being painted in French green as seen so often during this period. (Cnel.Av. Agustin Pasmor via Antonio Luis Sapienza)

LEFT: Pilots of the Primera Escuadrilla de Reconocimiento y Bombardeo standing before a Potez 25T.O.E. at Isla Poí in 1932. Note the distinctive arrangement of the radiators as compared to the earlier Potez 25A.2s. (Cnel Av. Augustin Pasmor via Antonio Luis Sapienza).

RIGHT:A Paraguayan Potez 25A.2 at the main Paraguayan air field at Ñu-Guazú aerodrome near Asunción in 1932, near the start of intense hostilities. Just to the left are the wings of one of the ancient S.A.M.L. A.3s left over from the 1922 revolution and, behind the Potez, an aircraft appearing to bear French civil markings. (Cnel Av. Agustin Pasmor via Antonio Luis Sapienza)

LEFT: A trio of Wibault 73C.1s in the field at Isla Poí in September 1932, showing the very crude conditions at the forward base. Closest is No.5, with what appears to be No.23 behind it, wearing a serial not otherwise recorded. (Museo de Historia Militar via Antonio Luis Sapienza)

RIGHT: The first pursuit type to see action for Bolivia had been the surviving Vickers Type 143 'Bolivian Scout', six of which had arrived in December 1929. Here, serial number '8' poses in full markings at Villa Montes in 1932. Being very nimble, it often out flew the Paraguayan Wibaults.
(via Ramiro Molina Alanes)

ABOVE: Tte. Doldan poses in 1932 before a Wibault 73C.1, apparently in front of the hangar of the fighter unit at Ñu-Iguazú aerodrome. The Wibaults proved very disappointing in service. In the background the titles on the hangar read Grupo de Aviación, 11 Escuadron de Caza. (Prof. Carlos Pusineri via Antonio Luis Sapienza)

ABOVE: The Condor Boliviano adorned the fuselage of at least two of the Vickers Type 143s during the early stages of the Chaco campaign. In this case, it is about to descend on Leon Guarani (the Paraguayan Lion), the face of which appears to be a good rendition of General José Félix Estigarribia! (Ramiro Molina Alanes)

RIGHT: Amongst the most important Bolivian aircraft during the initial phase of combat operations again Paraguayan forces were the survivors of the ungainly Vickers Vespa multi-purpose aircraft. Here, Bolivian crews pose with W.H.R. Banting, chief instructor on the type, at El Alto.
(Janes' All the World's Aircraft)

LEFT: Bolivia acquired at least six Vickers Vespa IIIs from Britain in April 1929, and although optimized for high-altitude operations, they gave a good account of themselves in the Chaco before being largely replaced by U.S. Curtiss types.
(via E. B. Morgan)

LEFT/ABOVE: Two views of a brand-new Curtiss-Wright C14R Osprey at the Curtiss-Wright St. Louis factory prior to delivery. The aircraft carries full Bolivian markings, aside from an individual serial number, and underwing bomb racks. (Curtiss-Wright)

ABOVE: A late war photograph of a Bolivian Curtiss Cyclone Falcon, with Osprey No.91 visible in the background. By then, the streamlined wheel spats had been disposed of, as had the cumbersome canopy over the pilot's cockpit. Note the much abbreviated belly slip tank on this aircraft, probably from a Hawk, and the tidy uniform of Tte. Alberto Paz Soldan.
(via Ramiro Molina Alanes)

ABOVE: In-flight views of aircraft of the Chaco War are extremely rare. Here, one of the ubiquitous Bolivian Curtiss-Wright C14R Ospreys is photographed whilst attacking Paraguayan troop concentrations in 1933 or 1934. (Museo de Historia Militar via Antonio Luis Sapienza)

ABOVE: Following delivery and assembly at La Paz, the new Curtiss-Wright C14R Ospreys were rushed to Villa Montes for further action in support of the hard-pressed ground forces. This trio appears to have had their engine cowls painted black already, but no serials have as yet been added to the fins.
(via Ramiro Molina Alanes)

Curtiss-Wright C14R Osprey, Fuerza Aérea Boliviana, La Paz or Villa Montes, 1933-34

ABOVE: One of the earliest known photographs of a Bolivian Curtiss Hawk II, showing no evidence of a fuselage roundel, but with the belly auxiliary slip tank in place. (George von Roitberg)

ABOVE:Paraguayan troops examine the remains of a Bolivian Curtiss-Wright C14R Osprey, almost certainly No.78 which was shot down in flames with the loss of Bolivia's leading "ace", Major Rafael Pabon and his gunner Sof. Mario Calvo on August 12, 1934. (Leigh Wade Collection, USAF Academy Archives)

ABOVE: The bombs being mounted on the A-3 racks of Bolivian serial number 44 appear to be British, and may be heavier than recommended for the racks. Bolivia acquired, along with the other Vickers arms and aircraft, a substantial quantity of aircraft bombs for the Vickers Vespa IIIs. Apparently, the supply of bombs last longer than the aircraft. (Library of Congress)

ABOVE/RIGHT: The desperate defense of Villa Montes, in which aircraft of the Bolivian air arm played such a pivotal role, is exemplified by the hazardous 'engine running' maintenance being carried out on serial number 42, which was awaiting the fitting of four more bombs.
(Library of Congress)

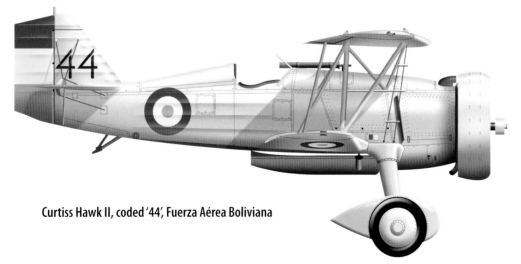

Curtiss Hawk II, coded '44', Fuerza Aérea Boliviana

LEFT: A close-up view of a Bolivian ground crew straining to secure a bomb on the A-3 wing rack of a Curtiss Hawk II. The A-3 could take as many as five smaller caliber bombs. (Library of Congress).

ABOVE: Although of poor contrast, a Paraguayan trooper's view of a Bolivian Curtiss Hawk II just after delivering an attack, reveals the extremely nimble maneuverability of this classic aircraft type.
(Library of Congress)

RIGHT : The two Paraguayan Potez 25A.2s, serial numbers '5' and '6', that were engaged by a Bolivian Vickers Type 143 fighter and a Breguet 19 in December 1932. Number '6' was shot down by Pabon, flying the Vickers. (Tte. Gonzalo Palau via Antonio Luis Sapienza)

ABOVE: As quickly as they could be delivered, assembled and tested, a new batch of eight Potez 25T.O.E.s were sent to the front in late 1932. The Potez aircraft were inferior in many respects to the newer Curtiss aircraft being fielded by Bolivia, but the tactics and skilled handling displayed by the Paraguayan crews made aerial engagements nearly always a draw.
(Cnel Av. Agustin Pasmor via Antonio Luis Sapienza).

ABOVE: Crews of the Paraguayan Segunda Escuadrilla de Reconocimiento y Bombardeo pose in their sweltering flying suits before a Potez 25T.O.E. at Isla Poí just before an operation in 1933. Note the length of the twin rear guns, accentuated by the stocks. (Cnel Av. Agustin Pasmor via Antonio Luis Sapienza)

ABOVE: Field maintenance on Paraguayan aircraft at Isla Poí consisted mainly of locating two stout trees just the right distance apart! On the right was (then) Tte. Agustin Pasmor, maintenance chief, who clearly worked with the troops. The aircraft is a Potez 25.
(Museo de Historia Militar via Antonio Luis Sapienza)

ABOVE: Paraguayan Potez 25T.O.E. serial number '12' returning from a mission in 1933. Note that the under-wing national insignia appear to include stars superimposed over the tri-color roundels. (via Antonio Luis Sapienza)

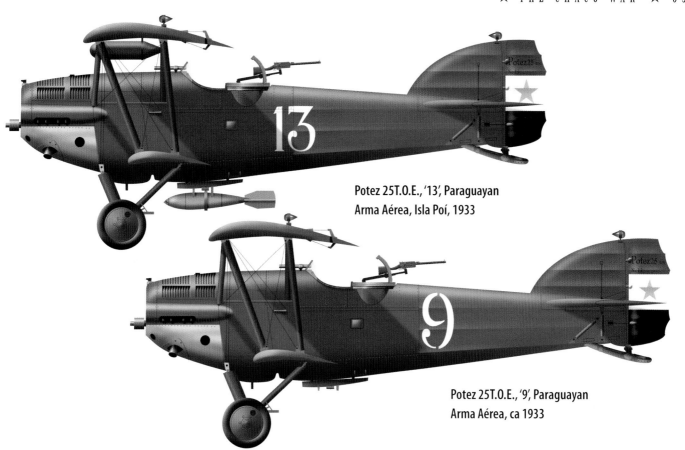

Potez 25T.O.E., '13', Paraguayan
Arma Aérea, Isla Poí, 1933

Potez 25T.O.E., '9', Paraguayan
Arma Aérea, ca 1933

ABOVE: The twin Madsen guns mounted in the rear gunner's cockpit of Potez 25T.O.E. serial number '13' at Isla Poí in 1933 reveal just how exposed the gunner was to the slipstream.
(Cnel Av. Agustin Pasmor via Antonio Luis Sapienza)

ABOVE: Although serialed in the trainer series as E-13, this Fleet Model 2 was photographed at the Isla Poí aerodrome in 1933. It had been acquired in Argentina around May of that year, and clearly had been crudely camouflaged, suggesting use in the war zone. The ever-present Tte. Agustin Pasmor poses with yet another of his strange charges in full field gear. (Museo de Historia Militar via Antonio Luis Sapienza).

ABOVE: During the last week of May 1933, a six-place Travel Air Model 6000 cabin transport was purchased in Argentina, and was almost immediately deployed to Isla Poí where it served in a multitude of roles as T-2. Note again the curious star insignia on the lower starboard wing. The aircraft appears otherwise to be constructed of doped aluminum. (Museo de Historia Militar via Antonio Luis Sapienza)

ABOVE: The disappointing Wibault 73C.1 fighters were replaced in March 1933 by five nimble Italian-built Fiat CR.20bis biplanes. This is one of the first examples received, still without its serial codes or unit markings. The CR.20s were unique in Paraguayan service in not displaying wing roundels; instead, they had red-white-blue chevrons on the wing extremities. (Museo de Historia Militar via Antonio Luis Sapienza)

RIGHT: Unlike Bolivia, which virtually re-equipped her air arm during the conflict, the only 'new' combat type to be integrated by Paraguay were her prized Fiat CR.20bis fighters. Here, Capt.P.A.M. Leandro Aponte, Commander of the Paraguayan Arma Aérea, stands beside a fully marked 11 Escuadrilla de Caza Fiat, Italian build number 431, in the field. (Museo de Historia Militar via Antonio Luis Sapienza)

ABOVE: The new Fiat CR.20bis fighters, all assigned to the 11 Escuadron de Caza, were immediately rushed to the front to fly escort to the hard-pressed Potez 25s. Here, Capt.P.A.M. Leandro Aponte poses for the camera in the extremely tight cockpit of one of the fighters. (Museo de Historia Militar via Antonio Luis Sapienza)

Fiat CR.20bis, No. 431, 11 Escuadron de Caza, Paraguayan Arma Aérea, March 1933

ABOVE: The remains of Paraguayan Fiat CR.20bis serial 11-1, in which Tte. Walter Gwynn succumbed to his injuries during a combat with a Bolivian Vickers Type 143 near Isla Poí on June 12, 1933. (via Antonio Luis Sapienza).

RIGHT: Paraguayan De Havilland D.H.60G Gipsy Moth T-1 was lost to a crash at Ñu-Guazú aerodrome on June 15, 1933, killing both crew members, Tte's Silvio Escobar and Alejandro Islas. Note that the entire rudder and fin have been used to present the national colors, and that there were no wing roundels evident. The aircraft was in the transport rather than trainers serial series, which implies that it may have seen duty near the front. (Cnel. Enrique Dentice, via Antonio Luis Sapienza).

ABOVE: Until recently, it was believed that Paraguay acquired and operated only two former U.S. civil Travel Air 6000 transports. This aircraft, marked with Red Cross ambulance markings and the serial number T-5, however, suggests that a third example must have been acquired, as it has been previously unreported. Here, it is seen preparing to evacuate wounded at Isla Poí in July 1933. (Library of Congress)

ABOVE: Another Travel Air Model 6000 that gained fame was the former Inter-Cities Airlines S-6000-B msn 6B-2011 (NC-624K), coded T-9 with Red Cross markings and named Nanawa. Tte.1º Emilio Nudelman (left) and Mayor (Dr) Silvio Lofruscio (sanitary chief of the Paraguayan Army) pose before the aircraft at Isla Poí just before an evacuation flight. (Ministerio de Defensa)

The Junkers K 43h monoplane combat aircraft ordered by Bolivia around October 1933, but not available for combat until around March 1934, were the most modern aircraft to see action during the war. This camouflaged example, with bomb racks under the wings, is seen behind the smartly-uniformed Capt. Eleodoro Nery, Mayor Jorge Jordán and Tte. J. Antonio Rivera just prior to action in support of Fortín Ballivian in 1934. (via Ramiro Molina Alanes)

ABOVE: Most unlikely warriors, Paraguay acquired at least two Junkers A.50fe Junior all-metal light aircraft from civil sources in Argentina in 1932, and both saw use in the war zone as communications and light transport aircraft. Here, T-5 is seen at Isla Poí aerodrome in 1933 with Tte. Agustin Pasmor, chief of field maintenance, in the front cockpit. (Cnel.Av. Agustin Pasmor via Antonio Luis Sapienza)

RIGHT: A close-up view of the very exposed dorsal gunner's position, and his 7.92mm machine gun, on a Bolivian Junkers K 43h, confirming that the position was in fact capable of being armed.
(Library of Congress)

BELOW: The pilot enjoyed a canopy which slid forward over the windscreen to gain access to the cockpit of the Bolivian Curtiss Cyclone Falcons. This example has rather disproportionate rudder markings, and no evidence of wing roundels. It had probably just been delivered to Villa Montes when photographed. (via Antonio Luis Sapienza)

LEFT: Bolivian airmen pose before one of the mighty Cyclone Falcons near the front. This example appears to have had the engine Townend Ring painted, probably red. Note the three-blade prop. (George von Roitberg)

ABOVE: One of the aircraft probably seen by the U.S. Military Attaché during an unrestricted visit to Ñu-Guazú during May 1934, in which he apparently included in his summary as one of a number of "...old foreign aircraft," was the solitary Savoia S.52 fighter acquired by Paraguay in 1927. During the war, it was apparently used for reconnaissance, but spent most of its time at the training base. Note that it has a single machine gun mounted on the upper starboard side of the fuselage. It suffered an accident May 3, 1933, and was grounded, but was apparently still intact at the school when the Attaché visited. (via Antonio Luis Sapienza)

ABOVE: Mentioned specifically in a German analysis of the Chaco War was the single Curtiss D-12 Falcons which had been obtained during the war under unusual circumstances. Often reported to have been used only as an "unarmed liaison aircraft," this photograph clearly shows number 17 with a pair of Madsen guns in the rear gunner's cockpit, in this view at Isla Poí in 1933. (Museo de Historia Militar via Antonio Luis Sapienza)

ABOVE: Seldom mentioned in Curtiss deliveries during the war were three Curtiss-Wright CW-16E Trainers, which were sorely needed by Bolivia. They were apparently based at Villa Montes in 1934. (via Ramiro Molina Alanes)

Curtiss D-12 Falcon, '17', Paraguayan Arma Aérea, Isla Poí, 1933

LEFT: Potez 25T.O.E. number 15 was a composite aircraft, built from spares and the remains of number 8 by the Arma Aérea shops. On 18 June 1934, crewed by Tte.2° Homero Duarte and Capt. Job Van Zastrow (gunner), it engaged in a ferocious dogfight with a Hawk II flown by perhaps the most flamboyant Bolivian airman, Pabón. He claimed the Potez shot down, but it in fact survived. (Ministerio de Defensa Nacional via Antonio Luis Sapienza)

LEFT: Two tireless Paraguayan Potez 25T.O.E.s that saw extensive action in a number of combats during 1934, numbers 9 and 15, are viewed at their operating base at Isla Poí aerodrome. (Cnel. Agustin Pastor via Antonio Luis Sapienza)

ABOVE: Tte.1° Rogelio Etcheverry, the gunner on Potez 25T.O.E. number 11 who was credited with downing Bolivian 'ace' Mayor Rafael Pabón, flying Osprey No.78 on 12 August 1934. (Museo de Historia Militar via Antonio Luis Sapienza)

RIGHT: An unknown Bolivian Junkers aircraft is reliably reported to have been lost in September 1934, but has eluded identification. Amongst some of the longest serving of the Junkers aircraft was the W 34hi Vanguardia, formerly a LAB aircraft, which saw duty as both transport and bomber. It is seen here at Villa Montes in 1934, and survived at least into 1938. (Juan Arraez Cerdá)

LEFT: Another view of the Junkers W 34hi Vanguardia during the war. The person lying prone on the innermost wing root area is a woman, truly a novelty in the Chaco, as is the tie that the man standing is wearing! (via Ramiro Molina Alanes)

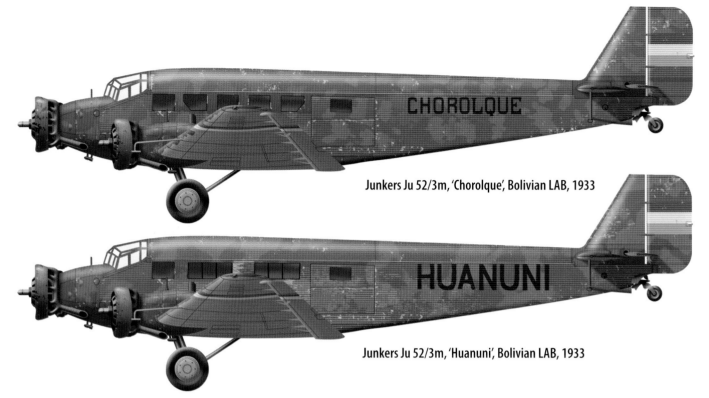

Junkers Ju 52/3m, 'Chorolque', Bolivian LAB, 1933

Junkers Ju 52/3m, 'Huanuni', Bolivian LAB, 1933

BELOW: One of the great advantages enjoyed by Bolivia through the height of the war were the LAB Junkers Ju 52/3m transports which were pressed into service to aid the war effort. This partially camouflaged example flew as far afield as Muñoz, where it was photographed in 1933. (via Juan Arraez Cerdá)

ABOVE: This view of one of the Bolivian Ju 52/3ms gives a good perspective on the rather unusual camouflage applied over all upper surfaces. It is believed to have consisted of green and brown splotches. (Hagedorn Collection)

BELOW: The hard-working Bolivian Junkers Ju 52/3ms were used to carry anything that could fit through the cargo doors, including this 75mm field gun carriage. This Ju 52/3m is also camouflaged, but differently from other examples. (Hagedorn Collection)

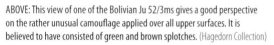

ABOVE: The sight of one of the huge Junkers Ju 52/3ms was an exciting moment in the Chaco. On the one hand, it meant the arrival of highly-prized supplies from the rear and, for the wounded, salvation. This example had the Bolivian colors in bands under the wings and on the rudder, and the engine cowls appear to have been painted black. (Hagedorn Collection)

RIGHT: Another stalwart of the Paraguayan Navy during the conflict was a single Savoia-Marchetti S.59bis coded R-1, seen here with her crew. It was the largest Paraguayan aircraft of the war. (Hagedorn Collection)

BELOW: This Paraguayan Navy Macchi M.18, complete with distinctive insignia, mounts a single Madsen gun in the bow gunner's cockpit at Bahia Negra in 1934. (Aviación Naval Paraguaya via Antonio Luis Sapienza)

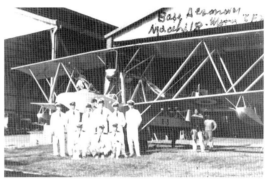

ABOVE: Used to great effect by the Paraguayan Navy during the conflict were two Macchi M.18 flying boats, including R-3 shown here. Note the trio of bombs under the lower port wing. (Hagedorn Collection)

LEFT: Tte. (later Capt.) Job von Zastrow, who certainly earned his pay as a gunner on Potez 25s, is seen here with a twin gun mount on a Navy Macchi M.18 at Bahia Negra in 1934. (Aviación Naval Paraguaya via Antonio Luis Sapienza)

LEFT: Ground crews of the Paraguayan Navy mount bombs to the underwing racks of a Macchi M.18 flying boat at Bahia Negra in 1934. These aircraft are seldom included in Paraguay's wartime Order of Battle by historians. (Aviación Naval Paraguaya via Antonio Luis Sapienza)

Macchi M.18, Paraguayan Navy, Bahia Negra, 1934

RIGHT: Neither side in the Chaco War had much time for personalizing their aircraft, although it is known to have occurred. Here, Tte. Enrique Dentice (first on left in flight suit) poses in front of a Fiat CR.20bis with "eyes" painted on the radiator louvers! The tri-color 'chevrons' can just be discerned under the lower starboard wing, unique to the CR.20s. (via Antonio Luis Sapienza)

BELOW: Paraguayan veterans of the Chaco campaign in April 1939 on parade. Shown are, from right to left, a Travel Air Model 6000, T-2, now named "Nanawa" (second use), a bare metal Potez 25T.O.E. without any visible serial, a Fleet Model 2, three Breda Ba 25 acquired after the war, and a mix of Fiat CR.20bis, CR.30s and CR.32s farther down the line. (Cnel. Agustin Pasmor via Antonio Luis Sapienza)

ABOVE: The sole Paraguayan multi-engine aircraft of the conflict, was a Breda Ba 44 T-15 which was used primarily as an ambulance, but also carried the Paraguayan delegation to the armistice meeting as VIP transport. Here, Capt. Emilio Nudelman (first on left) is seen at Villa Montes 14 June 1935 with a group of officers on the day of the armistice. (via Ramiro Molina Alanes)

ABOVE: An aircraft acquired by Paraguay and used extensively as a courier during the conflict was this Consolidated Model 21-C, often cited as a "PT-11". Definitely camouflaged, and with recognition bands inboard under the wings from the roundels, the aircraft was coded T-11 in the transport category and is not known to have been armed. (Museo de Historia Militar via Antonio Luis Sapienza)

RIGHT: Mentioned specifically in a German analysis of the Chaco War was the single Curtiss D-12 Falcon which had been obtained during the war under unusual circumstances. Often reported to have been used only as an "unarmed liaison aircraft," this photograph clearly shows number 17 with a pair of Madsen guns in the rear gunner's cockpit, in this view taken at Isla Poí in 1933. (Museo de Historia Militar via Antonio Luis Sapienza)

9 The Venezuelan Rebellion

Breguet Bre 19A-2, Venezuelan Aviación Militar, August 1929

Venezuela during the 1920s and 1930s was one of the most tightly controlled nations in the western hemisphere, and the regime of General Vicente Gómez went virtually unopposed between 1908 and 1935, with but one notable exception.

Gómez was extremely conservative, and permitted aviation in his realm to evolved only very slowly indeed, and under extraordinarily tight restrictions. In effect, the Venezuelan *Aviación Militar* (AM) of the period, almost completely controlled by a French aviation mission, came directly under his personal orders and it is no exaggeration to say that no airplane flew during the period without the express knowledge and consent of the *caudillo*.

By 1929, the AM had acquired a small batch of French-built Breguet Bre 19A-2 and Bre 19B-2 reconnaissance/bomber aircraft, and, with these, the first serious threat to the Gómez regime was thwarted in August 1929 when the Commander of the AM was ordered personally by Gómez to hazard the city of Cumaná, where the S.S. *Falke* had arrived bearing insurrectionist troops under *General* Román Delgado Chalbaud.

Although the aircraft did not locate the ship, they did attack the rebel forces in the city, with results perhaps out of all proportion to their effectiveness. With but two sorties flown, the Bre 19s were credited with stamping out the insurrection, and, with that action, cemented a relationship for the AM with the dictator that resulted in their enjoying a privileged position during the balance of his regime.

10 The Guatemalan Revolution

Potez 25A-2s, s/n 5, Cuerpo de Aviación Militar, ca 1929-30

Perhaps having witnessed the success of aerial operations in Nicaragua and elsewhere in the region, it is not surprising that aviation played a part in a period of internal turmoil in the Central American nation of Guatemala which erupted in early 1929.

Consisting of but nine aircraft of all types by the end of that year, the small *Guatemalan Cuerpo de Aviación Militar* (CAM) was ordered by the sitting government to attack several garrisons of regular Army troops within the nation that had risen against the Government. The attacks that followed were carried out by the most unlikely of aircraft types, mainly a brace of civilian Ryan B-1 Brougham aircraft using hand grenades, dynamite, and hand-held .45 caliber Thompson sub machine guns manned from the starboard front seat through an open window.

The download text describes the small CAM of the time, and its impact on the fortunes of the revolutionaries.

LEFT: None other than the President of Guatemala and Minister of War (in suits at center) were on hand on 15 July 1929, to witness the delivery of four French-built Potez 25A-2 reconnaissance bombers by the pilot Duroyon (fourth from left). At the time, they were the most modern warplanes in Central America. (Potez)

ABOVE: The four prized Potez 25A-2s were amongst the first aircraft to bear the now familiar Guatemalan star insignia, although it was dimensionally different from the modern version. (via Rick Ibarguen)

LEFT: A line-up of Guatemalan Army aircraft in August 1929 including one of the Morane-Saulnier M.S.147E.p.-2s nearest (probably No.60), two of the Ryan B.1s, and a Potez 25A-2. Note that the Ryans used the entire rudder and vertical fin to portray the Guatemalan colors. (via Rick Ibarguen)

LEFT/ABOVE: The two Guatemalan Morane-Saulnier M.S.147E.p.-2s, No.59 and 60, showing the large presentation of the national star insignia on the upper extremities of both wings. (Mario Overall and Rick Ibarguen)

ABOVE: First-flight of one of the Guatemalan Potez 25s, while a gun salute was taking place at right.

LEFT: The single Guatemalan Army Waco 10-T Taperwing. Note that the aircraft appears to have had some special insignia on the fuselage just under the rear cockpit, probably a momento of its long-distance delivery flight. (Mario Overall)

11 Internal Turmoil - Peru

1931 1932

Vought O2U-1E Corsair, '5-E-1',
Cuerpo de Aeronáutica Peruana, 1930

One of the four traditional great powers in Latin America, and beset by her own internal political divisions, it was perhaps inevitable that, as aviation came of age in this nation of extremes, it too would play a part in the social forces that sought change following the removal of strongman *Presidente* Augusto B. Leguía by a military *junta* in 1930.

Peruvian aviation by 1931 was, as in neighboring Chile, a strange consortium of Army cooperation and naval cooperation elements merged into a central organization known as the *Cuerpo de Aeronáutica Peruana* (CAP). Equipped mainly with U.S. built service types, the most effective of which were some relatively new Vought UO-1A and O2U-1E Corsairs, the service was called upon repeatedly to conduct what amounted to pin-point, precision attacks on small pockets of rebel troops or militiamen opposing Government forces. Although augmented by some armed Stearman C-3R biplanes, the Corsairs soon became instruments of fear throughout the Republic, as their mere appearance in the vicinity of a pocket of resistance was usually sufficient to quell or disperse the opposition. The download text describes the very diverse engagements in which these aerial operations occurred.

LEFT/ABOVE: Although marked with the distinctive "A-P" prefix (denoting Armada Peruana) ahead of its serial, 1-E-4, this float-equipped Vought UO-1A Corsair was actually part of the amalgamated Cuerpo Aéronautica Peruana (CAP). It was probably one of the loyal Navy branch aircraft that attacked rebel elements in Lima. (via Fred C. Dickey, Jr.)

BELOW: Rarely illustrated, this Boeing Model 21, A-P 1-E-1, was one of five acquired by the Peruvian Navy between 1924 and 1927, and is believed to have been used for observation during the internal turmoil period. (via Sergio Kaiser)

RIGHT: Peru acquired 10 Stearman C-3Rs as part of a package deal with United Aircraft Exports Inc, including 12 Vought O2U-1Es Corsairs, three Boeing Model 40-Bs and a Hamilton H-45 Metalplane in early 1930. Most of the C-3Rs were in the trainer series and were based with the Naval element at Ancon, such as 4-E-1 to 4-E-7 seen here, but also had the capability of carrying light armament and were used during the internal troubles. Note that the wings were painted yellow, and that the national insignia on the upper wings had a white outer surround. (Stearman)

ABOVE:The 12 Vought O2U-1E Corsairs acquired from United Aircraft Exports, Inc. in early 1930 were split between the Army and Navy elements. The Army aircraft, six of which are seen here, were apparently painted a dark olive drab, and were distinguishable from the Navy aircraft at the time in having six alternating red/white vertical rudder stripes. Serial codes on the fuselage were in white and included 5-E-1 to 5-E-12.

12 The Brazilian Revolution
1930 1932

Potez 25T.O.E., A-116, seized by the Constitucionalistas forces in São Paul at Campo de Marte

As can be appreciated from earlier chapters of this work dealing with Brazil, the decades of the 1920s and early 1930s were extremely turbulent in that largest of South American nations.

From 1922 on, Brazil endured nearly eight years of unbroken political turmoil, occasionally reaching the point of armed conflict. All of this reached a climax in the revolution of 1930, with the ousting of sitting President Dr. Washington Luiz and his replacement by Dr. Getúlio D. Vargas.

The Vargas regime almost immediately invoked a series of what were viewed as repressive measures, particularly in the industrial heartland of the nation, the state of São Paulo. A military governor for the state was duly appointed, and local political opponents imprisoned. The local – and very well organized and trained State Police organization – was summarily disbanded.

What followed has been without historical parallel in Latin American aviation history. While the Chaco War between Bolivia and Paraguay was continuing in the region, involving regularly organized air forces pitted against each other in modest numbers, the Brazilian revolution eventually amounted to nearly the same things, as the weight of the mass of the Brazilian Federal establishment was brought to bear against the state of São Paulo which, for all intents and purposes, was fighting as though an independent nation against what seemed overwhelming odds.

The Brazilian revolution differed also in scale. The sheer numbers of aircraft involved, operated by both Federal forces and the *Paulistas*, has remained without parallel to this day, and may be regarded from this perspective as truly the first Latin American conflict in which aircraft played a pivotal role.

The download text describes the nearly explosive growth in Federal land and naval aviation establishments, and the catch-as-catch-can acquisitions of the underdog *Paulista* aviation establishment, which carried on under extraordinary circumstances and, frequently, through convoluted international intrigue.

LEFT: Two of the 18 Morane-Saulnier M.S.147E.p.-2 primary trainers, K 129 and K 130, acquired by the Brazilian Army in December 1929.
(Author's Collection)

The aerial combatants in the Brazilian revolution benefited from a combination of factors that often challenged similar operations elsewhere. First and foremost, there existed a body of reasonably well-trained airmen and crews, concentrated in the two major population centers of the nation – Rio de Janeiro, the Federal capital, and São Paulo itself who were cosmopolitan, well-educated, often wealthy and fit. The aircraft involved on the Federal side were almost invariably current types of, initially, French manufacture, supplemented in very short order by an astonishing number of combat-adapted Waco sport aircraft from the United States that proved amazingly durable and effective.

The *Paulistas*, for their part, relied upon a varied assortment of civilian types volunteered or commandeered from the citizenry, supplemented by combat types in small numbers which were taken from the Federal inventory along with crews, who owed allegiance to their home state.

Between the commencement of hostilities and the end of 1933, the Federal air arm, the Army's *Aviação Militar*, alone had acquired

no fewer than 111 French aircraft – more than the combined total of aircraft operated by both sides during the Chaco War – and an even larger number of U.S. and British-built aircraft. The Federal naval aviation arm, the *Corpo de Aviação Naval*, for its part, the largest in Latin America, acquired a combination of U.S., British and Italian types, and together with the Army, posed a most formidable force.

From the beginning, the *Paulistas* were very much on the defensive, although there were a number of audacious missions which, in retrospect, read like the stuff of action thrillers, and the crews of these intrepid adventures were certainly not lacking in élan.

Like the Chaco War, the aftermath of the Brazilian revolution saw the introduction of a series of aircraft into Brazil that must have proved a quarter-master's nightmare, as, in particular, the Federals moved to bring overwhelming force against the secession of the *Paulistas*. These aircraft brought Brazil, at least on paper, to the forefront of military aeronautics in Latin America and, after the United States, made her collective air arms the most powerful in the western hemisphere into the early months of World War Two.

LEFT/BELOW: Concurrent with the purchase of the Waco 225/240/CSOs, Brazil also ordered 10 Waco CTO Pursuits, and although very similar, they could be distinguished by their tapered wings. Indeed, the Brazilians referred to them as the Waco Elipticos. Most examples were fitted with twin .30 caliber machine guns and A-3 bomb racks - they were essentially economy single-seat fighters.
(Waco via Stephen J. Hudek)

ABOVE: Views of Brazilian Army Waco CTOs in the theater of operations are rare. At least three of them were coded A-2 to A-4 for Ataque, and this image shows A-4 in company with Potez 25 T.O.E. A-117. (via Oscar Xavier de Fraga)

ABOVE: Rarely illustrated, the front cockpit of the Waco Model 225/240/CSO could be converted to fit two .30 caliber machine guns synchronized to fire through the propeller. The exact number of Brazilian Army aircraft converted with these kits is not known. (Waco via Ray Brandly)

ABOVE: The nimble Brazilian Waco Model 225/240/CSO aircraft could also be fitted with standard U.S. Army A-3 type bomb racks under the fuselage center line. More of these kits were acquired than the machine gun kits.
(Waco via Ray Brandly)

ABOVE: After the end of the civil war, most of the Waco CTOs were converted back to two-seat trainer configuration and given serials in the "K-" series. Here, K 254 still retains her twin guns and single-seat cockpit, next to K 257 which had reverted to a two-seat trainer. (Author's Collection)

ABOVE: Amongst the largest and potentially most powerful aircraft in Latin America at the time, the Brazilian Army acquired three twin-engine Loire-et-Olivier LeO-253Bn.4 night recon-bombers in 1930, coded K-611 to K-613 and individually named. As far as can be ascertained, none took part in the revolution of 1932, as few crews had been trained on them. (Author's Collection)

ABOVE: The Brazilian Army also acquired a mix of nine Boeing Model 256 and Model 267 fighters in 1932, as a direct result of the civil war. The Model 256s (essentially identical to U.S. Navy F4B-4s) were coded 1-101 to 1-108, and 1-103 is shown here after the revolution with the newer style Brazilian 'star' national insignia. The nature of the device at the lower right wing root is unknown. (Peter M. Bowers via Stephen J. Hudek).

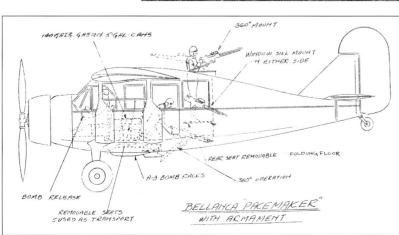

LEFT: An unusual purchase by the Brazilian Army, also spurred by the 1932 revolution, were two Bellanca CH-300 Pacemaker Specials. These were truly multi-purpose aircraft and, as seen in this drawing, could be armed with both flexible guns and A-3 bomb racks, a requirement for practically any aircraft in the inventory at the time. They were eventually converted to purely photographic aircraft as SGE-1 and SGE-2. (via Dave Ostrowski)

ABOVE: Another very significant combat type purchased as a direct result of the 1932 civil war was the Vought V65-B (often presented in error as V-65B), 28 of which were acquired by the Army, with eleven of them visible in this view from September 1933. (Vought)

LEFT: Amongst the capable aircraft acquired during the civil war by the Paulistas were a small batch of Curtiss D-12 Falcon attack aircraft spirited into Brazil from Chile during the latter stages of the revolt. (Author's Collection)

Curtiss D-12 Falcon, coded '3-110', Brazil, ca 1931

RIGHT: An impressive line-up showing virtually the entire Brazilian Naval aviation order of battle, as of late 1931, including six of the S.M.55As and the three Martin PMs. (SDM via Sergio Luis dos Santos).

BELOW: One of the most unusual aircraft to see action during the civil war were some of the Navy's 11 Savoia-Marchetti S.M.55A twin-hull flying boats acquired in March 1931. Here, serial number '3' rides at anchor in full Navy markings. Note a personal insignia on the nose and the small Navy roundel on the lower leading edge of the vertical fin. (SDM via Sergio Luis dos Santos).

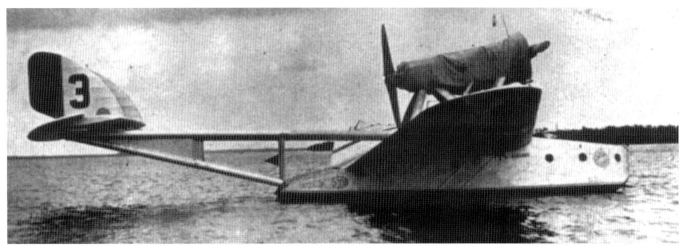

RIGHT: Used on numerous occasions during the civil war, the three rare Martin PM-1B flying boats acquired by the Brazilian Navy in December 1930 proved surprisingly durable and capable. Here, 1-P-2 bears a personal insignia on the starboard nose and bomb racks under the wings. (Author's Collection)

RIGHT: Loading bombs on the wing racks of a Martin PM-1B the hard way. Note the nose gunners scarf ring mount devoid of weapons, and the small national insignia. (SDM via Sergio Luis dos Santos).

BELOW: An deployment photograph showing Brazilian Navy S.M.55As and Martin PM's during the civil war. (SDM via Sergio Luis dos Santos).

RIGHT: Rarely illustrated, one of the surviving Navy Martin PM-1Bs post-war with the short-lived codes GM-P-10. (SDM via Sergio Luis dos Santos).

LEFT: Fighter pilots are the same everywhere, and this young nonchalantly posed Brazilian Navy pilot, was amongst the elite of his era. Evidence of a distinctive chevron on the upper wing can just be seen on the leading edge. (SDM via Sergio Luis dos Santos).

ABOVE: The six Avro 504-N, 185hp Lynx powered aircraft acquired by the Navy in May 1930 serialed 441 to 446 saw a surprising amount of service during the civil war. Serial 445, seen here, displays full Navy markings of the period. The odd streamlined fairings under the upper wing, often thought to be gun positions, were actually fuel tanks for the larger engine. (SDM via Sergio Luis dos Santos)

LEFT: The Brazilian Navy Boeing 256's soon sported distinctive insignia, and most operated with their auxiliary belly fuel tank, as seen here on 1-C-3. (Author's Collection)

RIGHT: Like the Army, the Navy also acquired six nimble Boeing Model 256 fighters in 1932 spurred by the revolution. Coded initially as 1-C-1 to 1-C-6, four are seen here deployed at a remote location. (SDM via Sergio Luis dos Santos).

BELOW: Not a large aircraft, this Brazilian Navy Boeing 256 serial number 1-C-4 seems to be almost 'worn' by her pilot! (SDM via Sergio Luis dos Santos)

ABOVE: These two Navy Boeing 256s are unusual in sporting color-coded engine cowls, apparently mimicking the U.S. Navy practice of the time. The aircraft on the left bears serial number 1-C-19, which was previously unknown. (SDM via Sergio Luis dos Santos)

LEFT: In full Navy markings, including the large red chevron on the upper wing panel, a Brazilian Navy Boeing 256 serial number 1-C-5 shares the line with two De Havilland D.H.60s and a Waco CSO. (Author's Collection)

RIGHT: Another previously unpublished Brazilian Navy Boeing 256 serial number GM-C-7 also bears, just aft of the serial, the unique Brazilian Navy designation/ serial presentation for the type, similar to U.S. Navy practice, C1B-33 to C1B-38. (SDM via Sergio Luis dos Santos)

ABOVE: Navy Corsairs operated on both wheels and floats. Here, late serial number GM-0-4 and GM-0-6 share the ramp with a float-equipped Navy Waco Model CJC. (Author's Collection)

BELOW: Fairey Gordon Mk.III 1-EB-4 on deployment with the 4ª D.E.B. of the Aviação Naval. (SDM via Sergio Luis dos Santos).

RIGHT: Numerically the most significant pre-World War Two Brazilian Navy aircraft, the 20 British Fairey Gordon Mk.IIIs which started arriving in November 1932 were very versatile aircraft. Navy Fairey Gordon's often flew in direct support of Brazilian Navy surface vessels, as shown with 4-EB-2 in flight over a Brazilian warship. (SDM via Sergio Luis dos Santos)

Fairey Gordon Mk.III 4-EB-5 in full Brazilian Navy markings, including upper wing red combat chevrons, in flight along the Brazilian coast. (Author's Collection)

ABOVE: Rarely illustrated, especially with "O" for Observação codes, this De Havilland D.H.60T Moth coded 2-0-3 was one of 12 acquired by the Brazilian Navy in 1931, and saw use during the revolution.
(SDM via Sergio Luis dos Santos)

RIGHT: Armed and ready for action, Brazilian Navy Fairey Gordon Mk.III 4-EB-6 carries six small caliber bombs on her underwing racks, but no evidence of a rear gun.
(SDM via Sergio Luis dos Santos).

RIGHT: After the civil war, the surviving Navy O2U-2As were re-coded 2-0-1 through to 2-0-6. Seen here in a lineup are 2-0-4 and 2-0-3.
(Serviço de Documentaçã da Marinha - SDM - via Sergio Luis dos Santos)

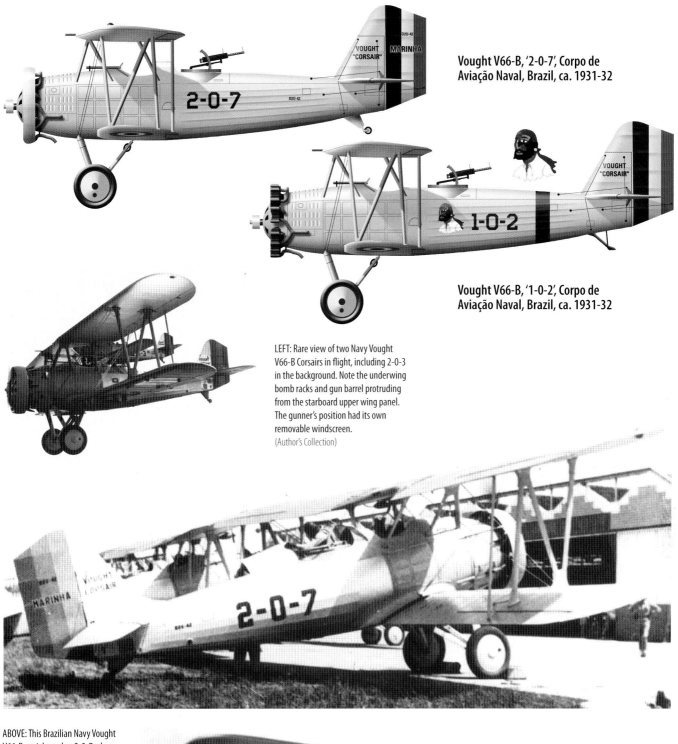

Vought V66-B, '2-0-7', Corpo de Aviação Naval, Brazil, ca. 1931-32

Vought V66-B, '1-0-2', Corpo de Aviação Naval, Brazil, ca. 1931-32

LEFT: Rare view of two Navy Vought V66-B Corsairs in flight, including 2-0-3 in the background. Note the underwing bomb racks and gun barrel protruding from the starboard upper wing panel. The gunner's position had its own removable windscreen. (Author's Collection)

ABOVE: This Brazilian Navy Vought V66-B, serial number 2-0-7, also bears the unique permanent service designator in smaller characters aft of the code, which were O2V-39 to O2V-46, also repeated on the upper rudder. (Author's Collection)

RIGHT: Crews restrain the wings of a Navy O2U-2A as a crewman ground runs the engine. (Author's Collection)

13 The Leticia Incident - Colombia and Peru

1932 1933

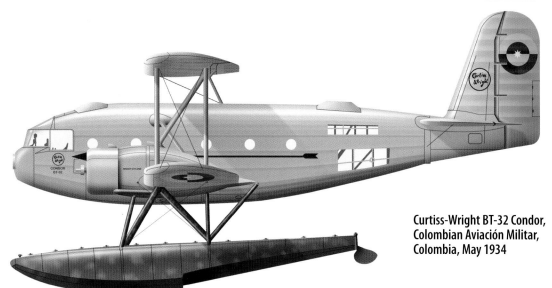

Curtiss-Wright BT-32 Condor,
Colombian Aviación Militar,
Colombia, May 1934

By 1932, to the casual observer in New York or London, it must have seemed that Latin America was afire, with the continuing, all-out war in the Chaco between warring Bolivia and Paraguay, and the bitter, internecine civil war in Brazil.

To those conflicts, starting in 1932, must be added the little-known and poorly documented territorial conflict between Peru and Colombia known as the Leticia Incident.

Started, as was so often the case, as a diversion from internal failings and as a focal point to rally patriotic sentiments, this affair was supposedly fought over an extremely remote and isolated tropical area of the Amazon backwaters known as the Leticia quadrilateral or trapezium. Although the Chaco region, contested by Paraguay and Bolivia, was certainly remote and hostile, the Leticia area, even by that comparison, remains difficult to match in terms of its inaccessibility and questionable value as a subject of conflict.

At the start, neither nation was prepared, from an aviation standpoint, to conduct operations in the area. Although both mobilized all available local resources, including, in both nations, all commercial aircraft extant, the ante was quickly raised as each scrambled to acquire, on a crash basis, aircraft and crews. Aircraft were sought which were capable of sustained operation in what was essentially an amphibious environment, and crews, which could be acquired or trained. These forces could then be brought to bear on the territory in dispute.

Although the total numbers of aircraft eventually acquired exceeded those flown during the Chaco War, only a comparatively few reached the combat zone in Leticia, and these only after extraordinary exertions. Peru faced the Andes *cordillera* (mountain chain) between its main operating bases near Lima and the Leticia forward bases, while Colombia faced nearly identical logistical challenges, although she arguably understood the necessity of float-equipped or flying-boat equipment better than the Peruvian leadership.

Peru elected, via the offices of prominent French and British missions, to acquire aircraft of mainly European design to face the Colombians. The Colombians, for their part, selected primarily Curtiss-Wright aircraft types, but also wisely took advantage of the highly competent German colony running their main national airline service, *Scadta*, and acquired very capable German aircraft types as well.

Although aerial engagements were rare, due to the extremely tedious supply lines, and the vastness of the area of operations, they did occur, and the download text describes these for the first time in detail.

As with the Chaco War and the Brazilian revolution, both Peru and Colombia, despite being brought to the table to hammer out a diplomatic solution, continued to seek armed aircraft as contingencies against continued conflict, and thus the fascinating aftermath is detailed as well.

RIGHT: When Colombia decided to go to war over the Leticia region, it had only 11 aircraft of all types, including several survivors of the exotic Swiss Wild WT43D trainer, serials 13 and 14 shown here, acquired in 1927-28.
(via Roland Eichenberger)

RIGHT: Colombia's Aviación Militar (AM) included amongst its equipment at the beginning of the conflict three airworthy Swiss Wild X two-seat reconnaissance-bombers. (via Roland Eichenberger)

BELOW: The first truly modern aircraft ordered by Colombia were an initial batch of three Curtiss Fledgling J-2s in July 1931. Capable of carrying two .30 caliber guns and A-3 bomb racks, they were underpowered as combat types. This example was part of the second batch acquired in June 1933. (Curtiss #W-8294 via Stephen J. Hudek)

ABOVE: The Curtiss Fledglings, despite their shortcomings as combat types, were exceptionally rugged trainers, and served the AM well to at least May 1950. This is serial number 18, one of the first three received in September 1931. (Col. Jesse Rothrock)

LEFT: This group of Colombian and U.S. contract pilots celebrate in front of one of the AM hangars after a graduation celebration, with a modified Curtiss Fledgling in the background undergoing an engine change circa 1936.
(Col. Jesse Rothrock).

BELOW: Peruvian aircraft on hand at the start of the Leticia crisis included at least two surviving Vought UO-1A Corsairs of a batch acquired in September 1927. They were most colorful aircraft, painted yellow overall which, with their red/white/red national roundels and rudder stripes, plus black service codes, made them highly visible. (via Sergio Kaiser)

LEFT: The single most potent aircraft available to Colombia at the start of the crisis was a single Curtiss D-12 Falcon, which had been acquired privately by famed Colombian aviator Tte. Benjamín Méndez Rey. Named Ricaurte, for a Colombian patriot, he completed a 4,600 mile delivery flight from New York in late 1928, sponsored by the newspaper Mundo al Dia. (via Richard S. Allen)

RIGHT: Ricaurte and her crew pose for the press on 18 November 1928, just before departing New York for Colombia. Although privately owned at the time, the aircraft bore full period Colombian national insignia. (Curtiss)

BELOW: Méndez and his back-seater, a U.S. mechanic, John T. Hunter (almost never named) mount the Falcon just prior to starting from the Canal Zone on the final leg of their 1928 flight. Although privately owned at the time, the aircraft was full armament capable. (via Jim Dias)

ABOVE: The flight of the Ricaurte was not without incident, however. The aircraft was damaged enroute at Coco Solo Naval Air Station in the Panama Canal Zone and, after valiant efforts by U.S. Navy personnel, was recovered, repaired and enabled to complete her historic flight. (via Joseph H. Weathers)

Curtiss D-12 Falcon, 'Ricaurte',
Tte. Benjamín Méndez Rey,
Colombia, 1928

BELOW: Relatives of the historic Douglas DWC World Cruiser's of 1924 U.S. Army Air Service fame, the Peruvian Navy acquired a total of four DT-2 torpedo bombers between 1925 and 1927, and 2-E-4, being beached here with a UO-1A in the background, saw limited use during the Leticia crisis. (via Fred C. Dickey)

ABOVE: For reasons unknown, at least eight of the 12 Vought O2U-1E Corsairs had unusual alternating white/red six-stripe rudder markings, instead of the conventional red/white/red three-stripe Peruvian rudder convention. They were otherwise dark green overall, and had the four-position national roundels placed quite far inboard on both the upper and lower wing surfaces. Fuselage codes were in white numerals and characters as was the type manufacturer/name on the vertical fin. (Sergio Kaiser)

LEFT: At least one highly versatile Travel Air S-6000-B transport was acquired by Peru, and modified to what was termed A6A configuration, as shown here. Coded 1-TP-2B, and float equipped, it made numerous important freight flights to the front. (via Nick J. Waters III)

LEFT: Representative of the odd collection of training and utility aircraft possessed by Peru at the start of the conflict, this single Travel Air E-4000 had a blind-flying hood over the rear cockpit (probably borrowed from the single Consolidated PT-3). It shares the line with an equally exotic Hanriot 18 H-438 trainers and a Morane-Saulnier parasol at the Las Palmas main operating base. This aircraft also displays the unusual CAP serial/code combinations used at the time.
(via Roberto Gentilli)

LEFT: As tensions with Peru escalated, Colombia began an almost frantic quest for competent aircraft to expand her tiny air arm. One proposed type, that nearly resulted in an order, was the little-known Martin Model 125 Llanero, a multi-purpose type similar to the U.S. Navy BM-1. Curtiss was able to offer earlier deliveries, and no orders materialized.
(Courtesy Dr. John Breihan)

LEFT/BELOW: Seeking a multi-purpose aircraft that could extend patrols into the far south of the republic to the Leticia region, Colombia placed an order for aircraft known as the Loening Type CE/CT in December 1931. The cockpit has two crew positions, a fixed forward-firing gun in a special fairing on the upper wing, a dorsal ring mount and A-3 bomb racks for various small and large caliber bombs. When the Colombians learned that Loening had used the aircraft as a demonstrator for other potential customers, the order was cancelled in October 1932.
(Author's Collection)

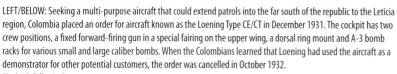

BELOW/BELOW LEFT: One of the first combat types acquired by Peru after the actual commencement of hostilities were Douglas O-38Ps. (McDonnell Douglas via Harry Gann)

RIGHT: O-38Ps were capable of operating on wheels or floats. 2-VG-3 and 2-VG-6 display this capability in this October 1933 view. The fin, horizontal stabilizers and wings are believed to have been painted yellow, while the fuselage was U.S. Army Air Corps blue. (via Paul Matt)

ABOVE: Rarely illustrated in service, the three nearest aircraft in this unique lineup, which includes three Fairey Seals and three Curtiss Hawks, all on floats, are the Vought V-80Ps coded 2-C-1E, 2-C-2E and 2-C-3E under the Roman numeral III. Note that by this point a black anti-glare panel has been added along the entire length of the upper fuselage of the first two. (via Sergio Kaiser)

LEFT: The two-gun armament of the V-80Ps was housed in a fairing in the upper main plane and did not require synchronizing gear, saving weight and increasing volume of fire. Upper wing and horizontal tail surfaces were painted yellow upon delivery. Since this photograph was taken in May 1933, it is clear that the actual order must have been placed well before then. (Vought)

RIGHT: Poorly documented, the three Vought V-80P single-seat Corsair variants that Peru contracted for in April 1933 featured a primitive sliding cockpit canopy. (Vought)

LEFT: Colombia commenced delivery of the first six of an eventual total of not less than 29 Curtiss Model 35-A Sea Hawk II fighter-bombers in October 1932. Here, a Sea Hawk on spatted wheel undercarriage shares a crowded hangar with several Curtiss Cyclone Falcons (including s/n 113) and a Fledgling J-2, s/n 17. (Col. Jesse Rothrock)

LEFT: The so-called "stage house" and wind tee at the main training base at Palanquero, with three Curtiss Sea Hawks, including s/n 810, on the line. (Col. Jesse Rothrock).

BELOW: Colombia was able to field her vast array of new aircraft only through the significant efforts of a number of 'contract' pilots of U.S., German, Cuban and other nationalities. Here, U.S. pilots (left to right) Noble (a USNR Lieutenant), Abe Peenstra and John H. Hayden (a 2nd Lt. In the USAAC Reserve), with mechanic Al Brubeck, await students, with a line shack and a Curtiss Sea Hawk on wheels in the background. (Col. Jesse Rothrock)

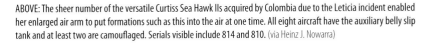

ABOVE: The sheer number of the versatile Curtiss Sea Hawk IIs acquired by Colombia due to the Leticia incident enabled her enlarged air arm to put formations such as this into the air at one time. All eight aircraft have the auxiliary belly slip tank and at least two are camouflaged. Serials visible include 814 and 810. (via Heinz J. Nowarra)

Curtiss Sea Hawk II, s/n 814, Colombian Aviación Militar, Colombia, ca.1932

BELOW: Seeking long-range bombardment aircraft that could reach the Leticia region and supplement the Dornier Wals, Colombia bought a single Consolidated P2Y-1C in December 1932 with a cruising range of 1,000 miles. Here, it is preparing to depart for Colombia on December 28th. (Consolidated)

ABOVE/RIGHT: After arrival in Colombia, the P2Y-1C, AM 611 (given in some sources as 610), was camouflaged. These views show the random application of the green paint over the doped aluminum and bare metal. Colombia attempted to acquire at least 11 more P2Y-1s starting in January 1934, but early delivery could not be assured and only the one was eventually acquired. Barely visible in one view, the P2Y-1C had at this point the simple three-color roundel (red/yellow/blue) mentioned in the text on the wings, and the more complex Colombian insignia on the rudders. (via Heinz J. Nowarra).

Three Swedish-built Junkers K 43do multi-place combat aircraft were delivered to Colombia around September 1932 as AM 401 to 403. Seldom fully armed, they were more often used as transports, similar to the configuration of 403 seen here undergoing pier-side maintenance. (Heinz J. Nowarra via George G. J. Kamp)

LEFT: Although most often seen as float-equipped, the Junkers K 43do's could also be equipped with a complex wheel undercarriage. Here, a group of Colombian and U.S. contract personnel, including radio operator "Baldy" Terrell, pose with one, which shows details of the underwing bomb racks. (Col. Jesse Rothrock)

ABOVE: Colombia also acquired at least five new-build Junkers W 34h transports (again, capable of carrying armament and conceived for wheels and floats) between June and September 1934. One of these, AM 408 crashed near Retiro shortly thereafter, killing one of the AM's great leaders, German Olano. (Col. Jesse Rothrock).

ABOVE: Between March and May 1933 the Colombians started taking delivery of the first batch of sturdy Curtiss Cyclone Falcons, a total of at least 23 eventually being acquired. Here, one is shown just after roll-out at the factory, note the three-blade prop. (Curtiss)

ABOVE: Just visible in the detail on this float-equipped Colombian Curtiss Cyclone Falcon, taken May 1, 1933, are the blister mounts for two .30 caliber machine guns on the upper surfaces of the lower wings. (Curtiss W-8151)

ABOVE: Colombian Curtiss Cyclone Falcon AM 117 with an auxiliary belly fuel slip tank. Note that this example does not have the peculiar half-canopy cover but, rather, two fairly standard windscreens for both cockpits. There is no evidence of underwing bomb racks and the gun port in the starboard wing has been taped over, indicating possible use as a transition trainer. (Col. Jesse Rothrock)

Curtiss Cyclone Falcon, Colombian Aviación Militar, Colombia, ca.1933

RIGHT: Showing details of the unique camouflage scheme applied to a number of the U.S. and German aircraft acquired by Colombia during the war - essentially green splotches sprayed over the doped aluminum or bare metal - this float-equipped Sea Hawk, flown by U.S. pilot Wackowitz, crashed into Cartagena Bay in June 1934 when the pilot fell out of the aircraft while performing aerobatics; he had not fastened his safety belts! (Col. Jesse Rothrock)

LEFT: Bearing the full camouflage treatment of the war zone, Curtiss Cyclone Falcon serial AM 111a indicates the second use of this serial. The forward sliding canopy cover has been removed, bomb racks are in place, but there is no evidence of wing guns. (Heinz J. Nowarra via George G. J. Kamp)

BELOW: Close-up look at the camouflage pattern on one of the Colombian Curtiss Cyclone Falcons, and the position of the underwing bomb racks. The forward sliding canopy has been removed. The U.S. crew, Jesse Rothrock and Noble, had just returned from a reconnaissance mission in the Leticia region. (Col. Jesse Rothrock).

RIGHT: Colombian Cyclone Falcon serial 111a once again, showing the random camouflage scheme from above. The national insignia are on the wing extremities, as well as on either side of the rudder. (Heinz J. Nowarra via George G. J. Kamp)

Curtiss Cyclone Falcon, s/n 111a, Colombian Aviación Militar, Colombia, ca.1933

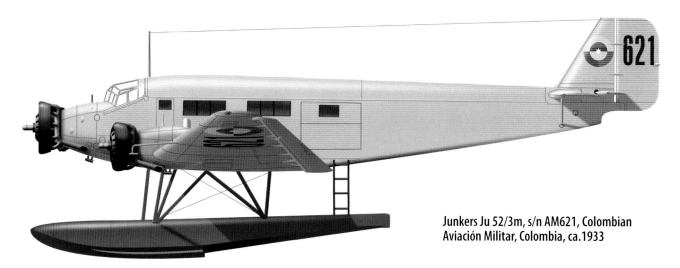

Junkers Ju 52/3m, s/n AM621, Colombian Aviación Militar, Colombia, ca.1933

RIGHT: Colombia's trio of Ju 52/3ms gave long and faithful service. Here, 623 and 621 sit on their beaching gear at a neatly manicured base. (Col. Jesse Rothrock).

LEFT: Unbeknownst to the Colombians, the Curtiss-Wright Export Corporation had also sold three Curtiss Sea Hawk IIs to the Peruvians, which had been delivered by January 1933. Also operated on floats, the Peruvians expressed dissatisfaction with their operating qualities. However this is believed to have been due to the low-octane fuel used. Here, 1-C-1B is tied up near Iquitos with one of the Hamilton H-45s in the background. (via Dr. Roberto Gentilli)

ABOVE: This view of a Peruvian Curtiss Sea Hawk II shows that it has been painted in an unknown color. As the red/white/red rudder stripes are clearly darker, it is assumed to have been a green color similar to that used on the O2U-1E Corsairs. The codes on the fuselage side are clear.

Curtiss Sea Hawk II, coded 'I/IVF-I', Cuerpo de Aeronáutica Peruana, ca.1933

ABOVE: In its own quest for combat-worthy aircraft, Peru turned to Europe and, amongst other types acquired were six Fairey Fox IIs (IV). The forward section of the fuselage, from the cockpit area appears to have been painted a dark color and has been decorated with a shark's mouth!

ABOVE: Amongst a 35 aircraft deal landed by French brokers for Peru during the war, were six rather angular Hanriot H-438 advanced trainer/general purpose aircraft with 240hp Lorraine engines. These were coded strangely, one having been 4/6-VE-4. These aircraft were armament capable.

ABOVE: The largest element of the French package was 12 Potez 39A-2 reconnaissance-bomber parasol monoplanes. The Peruvians had high hopes for these angular aircraft. Here, at least nine of them are on line and at least that many are known to have been in flight at once. (Potez)

LEFT: Fears of renewed hostilities spurred Colombia to seek additional multi-purpose aircraft. The first of 18 Consolidated Model 21s (marked on their rudders as "PT11C") arrived in March 1934 and, although ostensibly advanced trainers, had armament capability.
(General Dynamics/Convair)

ABOVE: As with nearly every aircraft acquired by Colombia during the Leticia period, the Consolidated Model 21s also had to be able to operate on floats. Note the added ventral fin attachment for water handling.
(Consolidated via Peter M. Bowers)

RIGHT: In AM service, the 18 Consolidated Model 21/PT11Cs carried serials 30 to 47 in numerals on the upper rudder (as on AM 32 shown here) and on the fuselage. They additionally dispensed with the black cowl and engine cover area of the prototype.
(Col. Jesse Rothrock)

ABOVE/RIGHT: Ordered well before the tentative armistice, Colombia took delivery of three Curtiss-Wright BT-32 Condor bomber/transports in May 1934. Shown here with the two dorsal "turrets" in place, and ventral positions visible in the lower rear fuselage, these were very much intended as combatants.
(H. G. Martin C-402-FE & C-1564)

BELOW: A strange group photograph, showing Colombian, U.S. and German aircrews freshly trained on the new Curtiss-Wright Condors after one had been converted to wheel undercarriage.
(Col. Jesse Rothrock)

BELOW: One of the mighty Condors, with turrets in place, is handled near the beach at Cartagena, next to a camouflaged Cyclone Falcon.
(Col. Jesse Rothrock)

ABOVE: The first Colombian crews qualified on the huge BT-32 Condor (qualifying on wheeled undercarriage first) under U.S. pilots named Hawks and O'Byrne - possibly nomes de guerre. (Col. Jesse Rothrock).

LEFT: Good view of one of the Colombian Condors on her beaching gear. The "turrets" were capable only of operating hand-held weapons and were traversed by using pedals. Note the bombardier windows in the lower starboard nose.

ABOVE: Never employed as bombers, the "turrets" were eventually deleted, although the aft ventral fighting positions remained. Here, FAC 651 wears the newer style Colombian rudder stripes and serial positioning. (Jerry Sympson)

ABOVE: Very rarely illustrated, the Colombian AM acquired three Fairchild 22-C7F aircraft via the Curtiss-Wright Export Corporation in July 1934, including serial number 50 seen here. (Col. Jesse Rothrock)

ABOVE: A pre-delivery view of one of the angular Colombian Bellanca Model 77-140s, the first two of which were not delivered until March 1935, near the factory in Delaware. (via Bob Esposito)

RIGHT: Photographs of the Colombian Bellanca Model 77-140s in Colombia are very rare. So far as can be determined, they never operated on wheels – only floats. This view, often claimed to have been taken in Colombia, was actually one of the second pair, taken in Delaware.
(via Fred C. Dickey, Jr.)

LEFT: Acquired purely as transports, the Colombian AM bought four sturdy second-hand Ford Model 5-AT-B Trimotors in 1934 and 1935, at least one of which operated on floats. This one has the large letters of the previous operator, Shell, painted over with aluminum dope under the starboard wing.
(via Dr. Gary Kuhn)

ABOVE: The final combat aircraft order for Colombia attributable to the Letica Incident was for three (originally to have been 18) Seversky SEV-3M-WW multi-purpose amphibians. Although marked "1" to "3" at the factory, they gained AM serial numbers 181 to 183 in their rather disappointing service careers.
(via Dave Ostrowski)

LEFT: This view of SEV-3M-WW X15391 shows the difficult configuration required for landing the aircraft, and the height of the pilot above the ground, a common complaint in Colombian service. (via Bob Esposito)

LEFT: The SEV-3M-WWs appeared far more at home on their floats and in the water than perched high on their problematic retractable wheels. This example still bears its test license, X15391, in New York. The exact nature of the armament on these aircraft is debatable.
(via Bob Esposito)

ABOVE: Unbeknownst to Colombia, Peru also acquired examples of the Curtiss Cyclone Falcon via the Curtiss-Wright Export Corp. as a result of the Leticia Incident. Rarely illustrated, this example tied up near Iquitos wears full service insignia and codes. (via Dr. Roberto Gentilli)

RIGHT: The solitary Caproni Ca 113 'fighter' - actually a very nimble aerobatics trainer, was acquired by Peru as a result of the war. One of the Ca 135 medium bombers which followed later can be seen in the right background. (via Sergio Kaiser)

ABOVE: Peru ordered 12 Caproni Ca 111 transport/bombers right off the Regia Aeronautica production line, accepting even standard Italian color schemes to expedite delivery in June 1934. Some were apparently second hand, as evidence of the Italian Fasci insignia seen on this example being unloaded at Callao.(via Dr. Roberto Gentilli)

ABOVE: Bomb racks can just be seen on the belly of this Peruvian Ca 111 as it moves under power off Callao, with an almost standard Italian colonial paint scheme. (via Achille Rastelli)

ABOVE: Nine U.S. crewmen and a Cuban pose at Cartagena in July 1934. From left to right they are Leon "Baldy" Terrell, Patterson, Brewster, Olin K. Haley, Mayor Terry (a Cuban), Wackowitz, Jesse Rothrock, Chappel and Kent. (Col. Jesse Rothrock)

14 Cuban Revolutianary Activity

1931 1934

Vought O2U-1A Corsair, coded '33', Cuerpo de Aviación, Ejercito de Cuba, Cuba, ca 1931

While momentous events were unfolding in the Chaco, Brazil and the Leticia region, Cuban internal politics of the early 1930s were, to a much smaller extent, marred by intermittent periods of revolutionary activity as well, and the small *Cuerpo de Aviación, Ejercito de Cuba* was called upon to play a part.

Equipped entirely with U.S.-built aircraft, the small service, cream of the Cuban military establishment at the time, was mounted almost exclusively on a number of Vought O2U-1A and O2U-3A Corsairs and virtually unique Curtiss P-6S Hawks.

Although seemingly of limited effectiveness, the attacks carried out by aircraft of this diminutive force were often credited with carrying the day for Government forces, and the download text describes these little-known actions in detail.

ABOVE: A formation view of CAEC Vought O2U-1A Corsairs revealing that, as of the time of the revolutionary activity on the island of Cuba, these examples had yellow vertical fins and yellow upper wing surfaces.

ABOVE: The principal aircraft involved in frustrating the 1931 "invasion" of Cuba by an expedition on Gibara island were a number of the Vought O2U-1A Corsairs, six of which had been received in May 1929. Note that the white star in the Cuban national insignia of this period pointed aft. (via George von Roitberg)

ABOVE: Cuba was the only customer for the so-called Curtiss P-6S Cuban Hawk, three of which were acquired in January 1930. This pre-delivery view of serial number 16, one of the aircraft involved in the attacks on the rebels, shows the rather bulbous forward fuselage and strengthened undercarriage unique to this limited Wasp-powered variant of the famous Hawk family. (Diz Dean)

ABOVE: Taken late in the revolutionary period, Curtiss P-6S Cuban Hawk serial number 18 had yellow upper surfaces on both wings and horizontal tail surfaces. The serial was carried only on the fuselage and the insignia just barely visible on the fuselage is unidentified. (via Peter M. Bowers)

The Uruguayan Revolution

1935

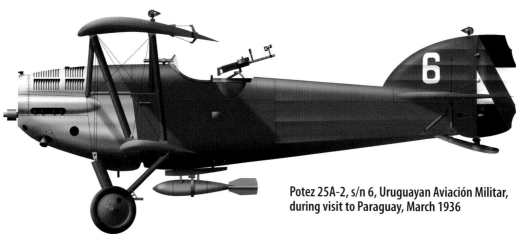

Potez 25A-2, s/n 6, Uruguayan Aviación Militar, during visit to Paraguay, March 1936

T he generally pacific Republic of Uruguay, often cited as the 'Switzerland of Latin America', endured an eight year regime by *Presidente Dr.* Gabnekl Terra between 1931 and 1938, sometimes cited as the "machete dictatorship". Eventually there were efforts to overthrow his cruel regime in January 1935.

Operating from bases in neighboring Brazil, opposition forces were met by a number of aircraft of the Uruguayan *Aviación Militar* (AM) at the behest of the Terra regime, which successfully attacked the insurgents and forced them to break up into small bands. Using French built Potez 25A-2s, a type prominent on the Paraguayan side during the Chaco War and in Brazilian Federal hands during the revolution just ended there, as well as some armed de Havilland D.H.82 Tiger Moths, the small but efficient AM, aided by civil aircraft impressed by the Army in early February, effectively observed the movements of the dispirited rebel bands and forced their eventual dispersal.

ABOVE: The venerable Potez 25A-2 once again saw action in Latin America with Uruguay's Aviación Militar during the short-lived revolution in Uruguay in January and February 1935. Serial number 6, seen here, saw action against the rebels starting on 4 February. It is seen here in much the same color scheme during a visit to Paraguay in March 1936. (May. Fernando Díaz via Eduardo Luzardo)

ABOVE: Unlikely combatants, Uruguay's A.M. pressed some of the initial batch of De Havilland D.H.82 Tiger Moths into service during the 1935 Revolution as reconnaissance and light bombing aircraft. Serial number 18, pictured in 1940, wears a standard overall dark green scheme of the time. A Potez 25 is just visible in the background. The aircraft were later re-serialed in the 600 series. (Nery Mendiburu via Dr. Gary Kuhn)

Potez 25, s/n 404, Uruguayan Aviación Militar, ca 1944
Seven of Uruguay's nine dependable Potez 25's survived into June 1940, and during WW2 the survivors were reserialed as 401 to 407. These would have been amongst Uruguayan aircraft to defend her territorial waters had the Graf Spee sea battle closed into her waters.

16 The Peru-Ecuador Border War 1941

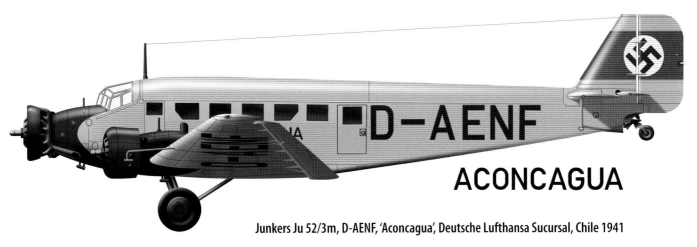

D–AENF
ACONCAGUA

Junkers Ju 52/3m, D-AENF, 'Aconcagua', Deutsche Lufthansa Sucursal, Chile 1941

As a direct result of the Leticia Incident, described earlier, by the end of the 1930s, Peru found herself in possession of powerful armed forces, with nothing to do.

Classic ingredients for adventures by dictatorial regimes, Peru found it expedient, through a number of questionable motivating factors (including an alleged German-engineered plot), to make border territorial claims against neighboring Ecuador which, comparatively, was militarily very weak indeed.

Equipped with an amazing array of aircraft from the four corners of the earth, including French, British, Italian and U.S. types in the majority, by July 1941 the *Cuerpo de Aeronáutica Peruana* (CAP) could count amongst its inventory some of the latest and most modern aircraft available in Latin America, including North American NA-50 fighter-bombers, Northrop 8A-3P attack bombers, Caproni Ca 111 and Ca 310 bombers, and Ca 114 fighters, and a host of other types.

These aircraft, formed into a combined air and ground force known as the *Agrupamiento del Norte*, launched what amounted to a *Blitzkrieg* type assault into Ecuadorian territory in early July 1941, and quickly overran the poorly equipped and sparse Ecuadorian defense forces in the area.

Although Ecuador managed to bring its few airworthy aircraft into the fray in a support capacity, the CAP enjoyed total air superiority over the area of the invasion and, by 15 September, Peru had achieved all of its objectives. It did so not without loss, however, as Ecuadorian anti-aircraft gunners, to their credit, gave a good account of themselves. This created a number of heroes for the CAP who are immortalized for their services to their homeland to this day, in spite of the questionable circumstances of their having been placed in harm's way in the first instance.

ABOVE: Seen in Chile on a disaster assistance mission while still bearing Lufthansa Sucursal markings and German registration, this Junkers Ju 52/3m named 'Aconcagua' apparently played a part in the commencement of the 1941 hostilities between Peru and Ecuador. (Lufthansa)

ABOVE: Taken at the factory, one of the modern North American NA-50s acquired by Peru, was an NA-16 single-seat fighter-bomber derivative. Note the bomb racks under either wing just outboard of the main gear.
(via Dave Ostrowski)

BELOW: A lineup of four of the highly regarded NA-50s in the field near Pizarro being armed for an attack on Ecuadoran positions. Three Caproni Ca 114s can just be seen at the end of the line. (FAP)

LEFT: A rare in-flight view of CAP NA-50 41-1. Note the combat chevron running aft on a diagonal from the leading edge of the wing. The pennant on the fuselage joins with another stripe around the upper rear fuselage, giving some observers the impression that this was a stylized arrow. The insignia near the nose was a unit emblem. (FAP)

BELOW/LEFT: A preserved example of a CAP NA-50 mounted on a plinth. The aircraft is displayed in semi-authentic colors and is now in poor condition. (Hagedorn collection)

ABOVE: The well-equipped Curtiss-Wright 19Rs could also mount an auxiliary fuel tank under the fuselage center.

ABOVE: The Curtiss-Wright 19Rs could each mount A-3 bomb racks under each wing.

LEFT: Rarely illustrated, the Ecuadorian Curtiss-Wright 19Rs featured .30 caliber gun blisters on each wheel pant, as well as one synchronized forward firing machine gun, and one flexible weapon.

ABOVE: The only modern types in the small Ecuadorian inventory were three Curtiss-Wright 19R all-metal light combat aircraft, which were hastily readied for service at the front. These included the first example received, named 'Patria'. Note the unusual tri-color bands on the underside of the wing tips rather than an Ecuadorian roundel.

RIGHT: The first Caproni Ca 310 for the CAP sitting just outside the Caproni "factory" near Lima, still bearing its Italian civil registration. To the left, one of the Ca 135 medium bombers is being assembled. As far as can be determined, they saw little use during the war.
(via Achille Rastelli)

BELOW: Another view of the Caproni "factory" at Las Palmas, with the first of a number of Caproni Ca 310s on the right together with a Ca 135 and at least one Ca 100 being assembled in the large hangar.
(via Achille Rastelli)

17 The SECOND WORLD WAR 1939 1945

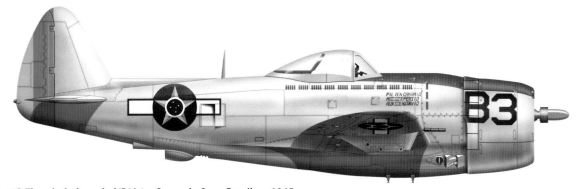

Republic P-47D Thunderbolt, coded 'B3', 1.º Grupo de Caça, Brazil, ca 1945

The extent to which the Second World War touched the western hemisphere and, for the purposes of this account, Latin America in particular, has somehow escaped a balanced accounting, and as a consequence, this chapter may prove especially revealing to students of that greatest of global conflicts.

Operations by the combatant powers in Latin America are included, since these very much affected the nations of the region, and, on the broader canvas, the war itself. Similarly, the wartime achievements of several Latin American nations – notably Brazil and Mexico, both of which sent units to active war theatres – but also other nations of more modest means, who also made contributions commensurate with their capabilities, are included.

Following the fall of France and the Japanese onslaught in the Pacific, for a time, the United States had to face the very real prospect of standing alone against the Axis powers. In retrospect, it was probably a combination of the British victory in the Battle of Britain, the disastrous German invasion of the Soviet Union, the failure of Rommel in North Africa and the continued neutrality of Spain and Portugal that forestalled what United States planners felt sure would be a German adventure into mainland South America, across the narrowest part of the South Atlantic from French territories in Africa.

Central to U.S. defense plans at this point was protecting the vital Panama Canal, as well as the approaches to that national asset and natural resources in the vicinity, not least of which was Venezuelan oil and bauxite from the rich fields on the northeast hum of mainland South America.

The account in the download text describes the U.S. aviation forces deployed for these purposes in the Caribbean region as of 1941, and the subsequent crash build-up programme that was assembled to meet the totally surprising and aggressive Axis submarine assault on the Caribbean that commenced in February 1942.

Engaging the U-boats, rather than meeting and defeating an expected surface or aircraft carrier-borne assault force bent on destroying or disabling the Canal, soon became the primary mission of the Allied defenders. To meet the submarine menace, the U.S. Caribbean Air Force (later redesignated as the Sixth Air Force) fielded a force that included Curtiss P-40, Bell P-39 and the ubiquitous Douglas B-18 twin-engine bomber, which soon became the premier yet unheralded standard-bearer in the war on the Axis submarines. The download text describes a number of the engagements involving the daring submarine commanders, and the Allied response in dealing with them.

U.S. Naval aviation, initially at a numeric disadvantage, by 1943 had been strengthened to the point where it was able to assume the primary responsibility for anti-submarine work. The torch gradually shifted to aircraft of that service – including both conventional land-based patrol bombers, flying boats, amphibians and blimps, some operating as far north as Cuba and as far south as Rio de Janeiro, Brazil, as well as west into the Pacific as far as the mysterious Galapagos Islands, where Army aviators had pioneered the way.

The download text includes a detailed listing of known submarine engagements, the aircraft and units involved, and the claims registered, for U.S. Army Air Forces, U.S. Navy aviation units, Royal Air Force, as well as Brazilian Air Force units.

Argentina, which remained neutral but sympathetic to the USA throughout nearly the entire wartime period, is described briefly, as her efficient military and significant economic and agricultural capacity could have easily influenced the course of events in the region, had her leadership elected to enter the war on the Axis side, as was widely expected.

Brazil, which besides fielding a highly decorated and exceptionally courageous P-47 equipped fighter-bomber unit to Italy to serve alongside the USAAF in 1944, also conducted a large number of unheralded coastal patrol and anti-submarine missions during the war. These are also dealt with at length.

Chile, another major Latin American nation with extensive natural resources vital to the Allied cause, shared with Brazil and Argentina the sensitive political issue of sizeable German and Italian colonies, numbers of whom displayed more than outright sympathy for the Axis cause. As a result, the U.S. bestowed considerable Lend-Lease largesse on the Chilean armed forces, who responded by engaging in largely ornamental coastal and anti-submarine and surface vessel patrols of its extensive coastline throughout most of the war, although the potential for Axis action was remote in the extreme.

Even Colombia, perhaps owing to her proximity to the Panama Canal, as well as El Salvador, Cuba, Guatemala, Honduras, Uruguay and even impoverished Haiti contributed, in their own small ways, to the war effort with modest results, and each nation established limited coastal and ant-submarine patrols to help unmask the marauding U-boats.

It is seldom recognized that Mexico was a genuine concern of the U.S. at the beginning of the war, since repeated alerts were sounded that the Japanese had intentions of landing an invasion force on the very thinly defended Pacific coast of that nation, and from there launch a drive north into the soft underbelly of the mainland U.S. Although far-fetched viewed from the perspective of 60 years on, the alarms that were raised and the extensive U.S. investment in mapping and documenting every airfield and landing ground in Mexico, as well as providing Mexico for the first time with state-of-the art aircraft with which to patrol her coasts, attested to the emphasis and very genuine U.S. concerns that existed at that time.

Mexico, like Brazil, desired a more active role in the war, especially after she suffered a number of unprovoked merchant ship sinkings in her coastal and Gulf of Mexico waters, a needless excess by the Germans that enraged the Mexican populace, as in Brazil. Late in the war, Mexico also fielded an active P-47 fighter-bomber squadron to the Pacific, to operate alongside U.S. forces there, and they served with distinction.

LEFT: Resplendent in pre-Pearl Harbor U.S. Army Air Corps markings, this Curtiss P-36A of the 16th Pursuit Group, stationed in the Panama Canal Zone and environs, constituted the most modern interceptors in the area as of June 1941. This aircraft was coded '16P33'. (Jim Dias)

ABOVE: This Curtiss P-36A of the 16th Pursuit Group's 43rd Pursuit Squadron, coded '16P63' (USAAC serial number 38-53) was highly polished, and was the pride of the pre-Pearl Harbor Air Corps defenses in Panama. (Jim Dias)

LEFT: The 16th Pursuit Group and 32nd Pursuit Group, represented here by a Curtiss P-36A of the 29th Pursuit Squadron, often deployed to Rio Hato, about 80 miles west of the Panama Canal, an important alternate base. The Douglas B-18 is from the 44th Reconnaissance Squadron. (Jim Dias)

ABOVE: USAAC 16th Pursuit Group Curtiss P-36As on the line at Rio Hato, Panama. The first aircraft is from the 24th Pursuit Squadron, the second from the 43rd. (Jim Dias)

LEFT: Curtiss P-36As, redesignated as RP-36As, remained on strength with the successor to the USAAC's Caribbean Air Force, the Sixth Air Force, as late as 20 June 1944. This was in fact that last one to serve in Panama, serial number 38-37, while serving in 1941 with the 29th Pursuit Squadron coded '16P34' at Rio Hato. (Jim Dias)

LEFT: Note the bisected nose cowl colors on this 16th Pursuit Group Curtiss P-36A and the 16th Pursuit Group crest on the fuselage. These, together with the three-color bands around the rear fuselage indicate this was the Group Commander's aircraft. (Jim Dias)

LEFT: Curtiss P-36As only slightly outnumbered Boeing P-26As in the Panama Canal Zone as late as June 1941 (17 P-36s and 14 P-26s). This 32nd Pursuit Group aircraft retains the classic pre-war blue fuselage with yellow wings and vertical fin, but additionally has had the wheel spats and cowl painted white. (Jim Dias)

LEFT: A third Pursuit Group, the 37th, was formed from cadres of the expanding Air Corps establishment in the Canal Zone, although initially very under strength. Here, six Boeing P-26As, two Curtiss P-36As and a Grumman OA-9 of the Group are seen at Rio Hato after activation in February 1940. (Jim Dias)

RIGHT: Seven Boeing RP-26As remained on strength in the Sixth Air Force as late as May 1943. This example belonged to the 32nd Pursuit Group as of Pearl Harbor, and has bomb racks under the center line, seldom illustrated. (Jim Dias)

LEFT: Never illustrated before, this Panama based Boeing P-26A was apparently adorned for some special occasion with very unusual condor's claws and legs. The insignia just aft of the cockpit is unknown.
(via Dave Ostrowski)

ABOVE: The most significant aircraft in the U.S. Caribbean defense scheme, numerically, at the beginning of the Second World War were 27 Douglas B-18s and 17 improved B-18As. Much maligned in the post-war press, the USAAC crews who flew them on anti-submarine patrols praised them. This B-18A was with the 25th Bomb Group (H) just after being deployed to St. Thomas in the Virgin Islands in 1941. (Herman C. Wood).

LEFT: The most modern attack aircraft available to the defenders of the Caribbean were 13 Douglas A-20As. These highly versatile aircraft figured prominently in early anti-submarine actions and this example, USAAF 40-120, survived to serve with the 23rd Tow Target Squadron in the Canal Zone by March 1944, complete with nose art. (Unit History, USAFHRA)

ABOVE: Along with other between-the-wars types, 13 Northrop A-17s with fixed landing gear were deployed to Panama, including 'HQ3' which was apparently assigned to Headquarters, 12th Pursuit Wing circa August 1941 for communications purposes. Note the two-color engine cowl. (Jim Dias)

ABOVE: Aircraft of the Sixth Air Force adopted camouflage schemes not seen in other theaters on USAAF aircraft, as on these North American O-47As of the 1st Observation Squadron which operated mainly on the Pacific side of the isthmus before converting to B-18s. (via Dave Ostrowski)

ABOVE: A very rare pre-war color view of one of the 39th Observation Squadron North American O-47As on patrol in typical Caribbean skies. (Vincent H. Smith)

RIGHT: Ideal for the lonely coastal patrols and inter-island reconnaissance missions peculiar to the Caribbean, this North American O-47A of the 39th Observation Squadron ('39Δ3') was one of 12 that initially arrived. (Jim Dias)

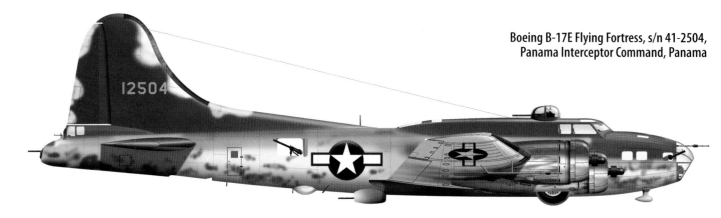

Boeing B-17E Flying Fortress, s/n 41-2504,
Panama Interceptor Command, Panama

ABOVE: As of June 1941, a solitary Grumman OA-9 amphibian was assigned to the 12th Pursuit Wing for transportation and air-sea-rescue duties in Panama as '12PW2', but otherwise in pre-war blue/yellow colors. It is probably 38-573. (Jim Dias)

RIGHT: One of the greatest boosts to Panama's long-range patrol force were nine brand-new Boeing B-17Es which started to arrive in June 1941, including 41-2504, which flew down in April 1942, seen here on a typical low-altitude coastal patrol. Note the radar antenna on the nose. (USAF 60563AC)

RIGHT: During the second half of 1941, Panama's defenses were bolstered by an influx of Curtiss P-40Bs and seven P-40Cs, including '59' seen here at the deployment strip at Agua Dulce, Panama. (John H. Peck)

RIGHT: By the middle WW2 years, the most common interceptor aircraft in the Sixth Air Force region were versions of the Bell P-39 Airacobra. This rather worn P-39K was a 29th Fighter Squadron aircraft, field number '24', pictured here at Albrook Field. (via Bob Taylor).

ABOVE: Another manifestation of the hasty camouflage painted on Caribbean based aircraft after Pearl Harbor, this 16th Pursuit Group Curtiss P-40B '16P44' was deployed at one of the many auxiliary fighter strips in Panama. (Maury Lauber)

ABOVE: The venerable Douglas B-18s, rugged as they were, could not always cope with the primitive operating conditions. This 1st Reconnaissance Squadron (formerly Observation), 36-291, became mired up to its wheel wells at Bluefields, Nicaragua at the end of a Caribbean patrol arc. (Jerry Sympson)

RIGHT: The arrival of MAD gear for the anti-submarine forces by April 1943 altered the campaign against the U-boats for good. This line-up of 417th Bomb Squadron Detachment at Camaguey, Cuba included a B-18A, 37-474 (although it has clearly been converted to B-18B standard) as well as two non-MAD B-18Bs, 37-559 and 39-24. Note the variation in the size of the US insignia but retention of turrets. (DIA)

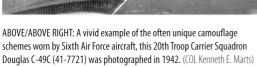

ABOVE/ABOVE RIGHT: A vivid example of the often unique camouflage schemes worn by Sixth Air Force aircraft, this 20th Troop Carrier Squadron Douglas C-49C (41-7721) was photographed in 1942. (COL Kenneth E. Marts)

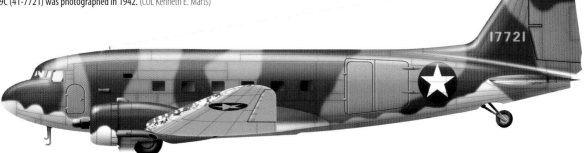

Douglas C-49C, s/n 41-7721, 20th Troop Carrier Squadron, US Sixth Air Force, 1942

ABOVE: The Sixth Air Force covered an immense geographical area, and as a direct consequence, had a constant requirement for transport aircraft of all kinds. This Fairchild UC-61, 41-38795, squadron number '5' bears the unique camouflage sported by aircraft of this hard-working unit as of May 1943. (COL Kenneth E. Marts)

LEFT/BELOW: The aircraft that became the solitary USAAF Junkers C-79 was none other than the Junkers Ju 52/3m 'Acaonagua' which played a central role in the the 1941 war between Ecuador and Peru. (COL Kenneth E. Marts)

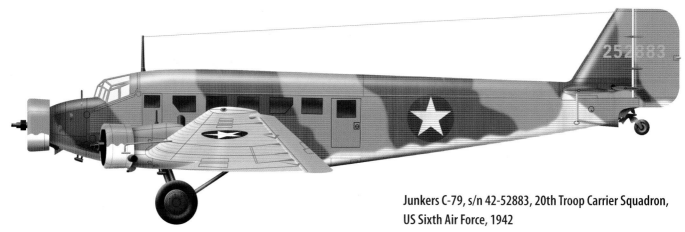

Junkers C-79, s/n 42-52883, 20th Troop Carrier Squadron, US Sixth Air Force, 1942

ABOVE: Desperate for anything that could carry cargo or troops, the hard-pressed 20th Troop Carrier Squadron found itself with the one-and-only Hamilton UC-89 by December 1942. It had been on the Panama civil register as R-12. The pilot appears to be holding his head in relief! (COL Kenneth E. Marts)

ABOVE: As in other war theaters, first echelon maintenance was often a very open air affair. The crew of this 1st Reconnaissance Squadron Douglas B-18A prepare the aircraft for yet another lonely, dangerous patrol. Note the .30 caliber machine gun in the lower nose turret mount. (Unit History USAFHRA)

LEFT: Seldom seen in formation, these three Douglas B-18As of the 12th Bomb Squadron flew much of their anti-submarine war from Guiana bases. (USAF 21363AC)

LEFT: The weary Douglas B-18s remained vital to the Caribbean anti-submarine campaign well into 1943, when replaced by more modern aircraft. The crew of 36-275 prepare for another long patrol, and the ancient gun turret is fully equipped with its single .30 caliber gun. (USAF)

ABOVE: Extolled for her service in the Far East early in the war, in fact the hybrid B-17D which came to be known as The Swoose received the bulk of her modifications and saw most of her wartime service in the Caribbean. Here is a seldom seen view of her namesake artwork on the starboard rear fuselage, at Port-au-Prince, Haiti, in March 1943. (Author's Collection)

ABOVE/RIGHT: Another one-of-a-kind aircraft to see very extensive service in the Caribbean theater during the war was the Boeing XB-15, shown here in 1944 on the Galapagos. It, too, was assigned to the 20th Troop Carrier Squadron. (Lt. Jack Schneider)

RIGHT: By the height of the anti-submarine campaign, the hard-pressed Sixth Air Force B-18s had been supplemented by small numbers of Consolidated LB-30 and B-24D Liberators, which proved ideal for the long patrols. This is B-24D 41-23662, which finally arrived in Panama in September 1942, pictured here in 1944 with the special night patrol scheme. (USAF)

LEFT: Although blurred, this is a very rare view of a 3rd Bomb Squadron Consolidated LB-30 Liberator as it lands at the end of the very long patrol arc at David, Panama, inbound from the Galapagos. The undersurface scheme is of interest. (via Chuck Meketa)

BELOW: As the demands of the more active war theaters eased, the long-range patrol elements of the Sixth Air Force finally received new aircraft. These included 12 Consolidated B-24Ms, including 44-51589, shown here with the night patrol color scheme used by aircraft operating from the Galapagos with the 29th Bomb Squadron. (Chuck Meketa)

During the early months of the war, U.S. Caribbean Air Force intelligence services kept a very close eye on several aircraft of Axis origins that were within striking range of the vital Panama Canal. These include:
(LEFT), a single Fiat B.R.20 operated by Venezuela as late as August 1944 (George von Roitberg), a small squadron of Caproni Ca 135s (BELOW), operated by Peru (Sergio Kaiser), a small number of Junkers Ju 52/3ms (BELOW/LEFT), armament capable, operating in Colombia and a bomb-rack equipped Curtiss-Wright T-32C Condor (BOTTOM), operated by Honduras!. (Author's Collection)

**Curtiss-Wright T-32C Condor, '7',
Fuerza Aérea Hondureña, ca. 1944**

**Junkers Ju 52/3m, coded '625', Colombian Aviación
Militar, Colombia, ca 1944**

LEFT: The array of aircraft used in Panama, which have intrigued aviation historians for half a century, included two Luscombe aircraft, including UC-90 42-79550 Junior assigned to Headquarters and Headquarters Squadron, Sixth Air Force, by 1944.
(COL O. C. Griffith/USAF Museum)

LEFT: During the initial German submarine attacks on Aruba and Curaçao, one of the first aircraft to respond was an armed Fokker F.XVIII of the Netherlands West Indies Defense Forces, formerly KNILM PJ-AIO Oriol. (via R. von Kolk)

ABOVE: MM3/C J. F. Connally excitedly describes to a Rear Admiral and an Army General how his PBY-5, 'P-1' of VP-53, sank a German submarine, U-156, on 8 March 1943. It was the first confirmed Trinidad-based sinking. The pilot, Lt. (jg) John E. Dryden, is third from right. Note the antenna array on the Catalina. (NARA RG80-G #73660)

ABOVE: From the autumn of 1942, aviation units of the U.S. Navy assumed ever greater responsibility for the air war against Axis submarines in the Caribbean and down the Antilles chain into the 'hump' of Brazil. This Consolidated PBY-5 Catalina of VP-92, coded '92-P-10' was operating from Guantanamo Bay NAS, Cuba, by May 1942. (NARA RG80-G #13377).

LEFT: Never illustrated in print before, this is the U.S. Navy seaplane base in the Galapagos Islands, from where very long anti-submarine patrols were flown over the Pacific approaches to the Panama Canal. The PBY-5 on the ramp has depth bombs on its wing racks. (NARA RG80-G #82719)

LEFT: A number of epic aircraft-versus-submarine gun battles were fought in the Caribbean and adjacent waters between German U-boats on the surface and Martin PBM-3 Mariners. This PBM-3, 'P-4', was operating from Natal, Brazil, as of April 1945, and is typical of the color schemes worn. (NARA RG80-G #49003)

RIGHT: U.S. Navy aviation in the Caribbean and Latin America was very small at the start of the war, but gradually built to assume a major share of the responsibilities which had been shouldered largely by the Sixth Air Force. An unusual aircraft operating in support of the Sixth's equally dispersed units was this modified Consolidated "PBY-5-R" based at Coco Solo NAS, Canal Zone, by 1944, BuA 1245. (NARA RG80-G)

LEFT/FAR LEFT: U.S. Navy anti-submarine units had received Consolidated PB4Y-1 Liberators by late 1944, including these two attractively decorated examples operated by squadrons of FAW-16 in Brazil. (NARA RG80-G #358578 & 358580)

RIGHT: The first U.S. Navy blimp to see service in the Caribbean was 'K-84' of ZP-51, starting in February 1943. It is seen here preparing for a patrol on 14 October 1943. Note the gun turret at upper right, and the depth bombs on the starboard lower side of the gondola. (NARA RG80-G #55198)

ABOVE: Argentina's Comando de Aviación Naval (CAN) had primary responsibility for coastal patrols during the war. A most unlikely patrol aircraft that was pressed into this role, was at least one of her Curtiss-Wright T-32 Condor's. (Author's Collection)

ABOVE: Until the arrival of Lend-Lease equipment, Brazil conducted very long coastal and anti-submarine patrols with an astonishing array of aircraft. These included Brazilian Navy Focke-Wulf Fw 58B-2s, some of which had been assembled in Brazil. (via George von Roitberg)

ABOVE:Brazilian patrol units also conducted patrols with Vultee V-11GB-2s when that country entered the Second World War. (via Dave Ostrowski)

RIGHT: Another patrol aircraft used by Brazil early in the war were some of her North American NA-44s (NA-72s), which were very colorfully marked indeed. (NAA via Boeing Archive)

ABOVE: Later covered retroactively by Lend-Lease, a number of Curtiss P-36As were sent to the 'hump' of Brazil from Panama under Defense Aid, and operated jointly by U.S. and Brazilian crews to bolster the defenses of that vital region. Here, '03' (formerly USAAC 38-43) is seen at Fortaleza in February 1942. (J. V. Crow)

RIGHT: With the Brazilian star national insignia painted on a white background disc, this is the North American B-25B Mitchell, FAB 09, that carried out one of the first Brazilian attacks on a German U-boat in Brazilian waters. (via Gustavo Wetch)

LEFT: Brazil very proudly fielded her own highly-trained anti-submarine Consolidated PBY-5A Catalina-equipped unit late in the war. Note the unusual combination of white fuselage on '14' and the U.S. Navy blue on the upper engine cowlings and upper wing. Although the crewmen were a mix of Navy and Air Force personnel, the aircraft were operated by the Air Force.
(via Sam Parker)

LEFT/ABOVE: Republic P-47D Thunderbolts, still bearing the markings they wore while in Italy with the 1º GAvCa, where they served with distinction.
(Magallaes Motta)

Republic P-47D Thunderbolt, coded 'C3', 1.º Grupo de Caça, Brazil, ca 1945

LEFT: Perhaps the strangest potential combatant of the Caribbean anti-submarine campaign was this Haitian Air Corps Douglas O-38E which came to grief on the harsh coastline during one such patrol in 1943. Note the depth charge which had torn loose during the crash landing in the foreground.
(MAJ Dean H. Eshelman via Jimmie Eshelman)

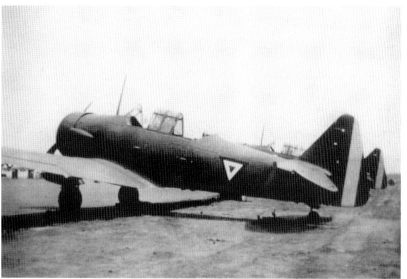

ABOVE: Colombia conducted anti-submarine patrols along her Caribbean coast using Lend-Lease supplied North American AT-6 Texans and Curtiss Cyclone Falcon's, which were referred by this time for reasons unknown as 'F-8s'. This example was based at Barranquilla as late as January 1944. (FAC)

RIGHT: Early in the war, Mexico's chief contribution to the cause was anti-submarine and coastal patrols from some very isolated locations. This pair of unserialed AT-6B Texans, armed with 100 pound bombs, wore olive drab camouflage from their Caribbean coastal patrol base. (Ing. Enrique Velasco via Santiago Flores)

North American AT-6C, coded '106', Cuerpo de Aviación, Ejercito de Cuba, Cuba, 1943

ABOVE: A Cuban North American AT-6C, CAEC 106, sets out on an anti-submarine patrol along her northern coast during the war. Note the very small caliber bombs suspended under each wing. (via Leif Hellström)

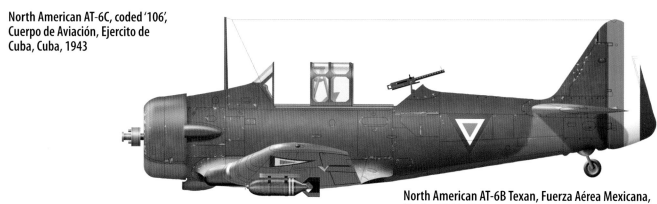

North American AT-6B Texan, Fuerza Aérea Mexicana, Mexico 1942-43

RIGHT: The all-Mexican 201 Escuadron deployed with U.S. forces during the retaking of the Philippines late in the war. Initially equipped with hand-me-down P-47D Thunderbolts, it soon received its own Lend-Lease P-47Ds such as 44-33722/"20" seen here in full unit markings. (Ing. Jose Villela, Jr.)

ABOVE: Besides an ever increasing number of AT-6s and older service types used on the extensive net of coastal patrols, both the Mexican Air Force and Navy received Vought-Sikorsky OS2U-3 Kingfishers for this and convoy escort duties. These air force aircraft have just been delivered, serials 69 to 74 in the old pre-war series (later OZS-4501 to OZS-4506).
(Ing. Enrique Velasco via Santiago Flores)

RIGHT: Rarely illustrated in color, Mexican 201 Escuadron Republic P-47D Thunderbolt 44-33721/"18" flies patrol over Allied warships near Luzon. Note that the Mexican national insignia was carried on the upper right wing and rudder, and the U.S. insignia on the fuselage and upper left wing. (NARA)

Republic P-47D Thunderbolt, 44-33721/'18', 201 Escuadron, Fuerza Aérea Mexicana, Luzon, Philippines, June 1945

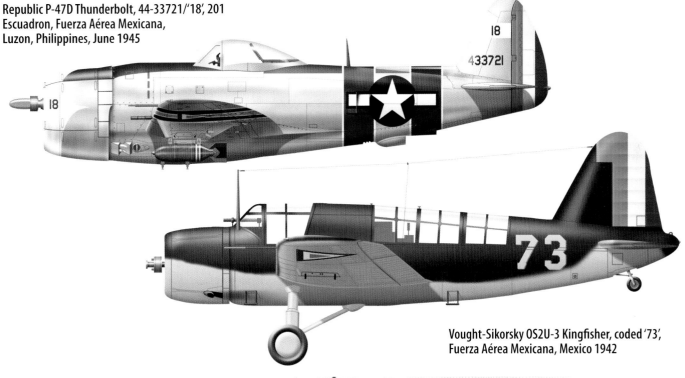

Vought-Sikorsky OS2U-3 Kingfisher, coded '73', Fuerza Aérea Mexicana, Mexico 1942

ABOVE: Another unlikely warrior in the anti-submarine war was the Honduran Stinson Model "O" Senior, one of which was lost under unknown circumstances while on such a patrol. (NARA RG165 #177-D)

ABOVE: Tiny El Salvador, in Central America, mounted an intermittent coastal and anti-submarine patrol along her Pacific coastline during the war years as a small contribution to the Allied war effort. Besides Lend-Lease North American AT-6s, one or two of the best surviving Bergamaschi/Caproni AP-1 attack aircraft were believed briefly used before damage to their wooden wings rendered them inoperable. (Author's Collection)

RIGHT: Across the river from Buenos Aires, Argentina, the small Uruguayan Aviación Naval conducted numerous coastal and anti-submarine patrols from bases near Montevideo. Here, pilot E. Falco and gunner S/O Alonso fly near the main operating base. Uruguayan Naval aircraft wore different rudder insignia than their air force counterparts.
(Juan Pedro Trabal via Eduardo Luzardo)

Vought-Sikorsky OS2U-3 Kingfisher, coded 'OP-2', Uruguayan Aviación Naval, ca 1945

Vought-Sikorsky OS2U-3 Kingfisher, coded '308', Fuerza Aérea Nacional, Chile, late 1942
Originally intended for the Chilean Navy, which had all but dismantled its aviation component, coast patrols were also flown by
OS2U-3 Kingfishers supplied to the Fuerza Aérea de Chile during the war, including '308'

18 Colombian Civil War

1946 1947

C-47A-30-DK, coded FAC 650, Fuerza Aérea Colombiana, Colombia, 1979

Beset by daunting geographic challenges, with widely dispersed and divergent population centers, World War Two brought only a temporary cessation of internal dissent in Colombia. No sooner than the Axis were defeated, than the nation soon launched into what, in retrospect, seems like an almost never ending series of internal disorders that have continued to the present day. These have since transformed into the devastating infrastructure that is fueling much of the world's appetite for illegal drugs.

In the beginning, however, the ideals that motivated Colombian rebel elements were similar to those expressed so often elsewhere: economic, agrarian and political reforms aimed at destroying or replacing the existing oligarchy, a perhaps simplistic but almost universal theme in Latin America in one form or another.

The Colombian armed forces, which had modernized considerably during and after the so-called 'Leticia Incident' with Peru in the 1930s, and which also benefited from Lend-Lease during the war and the replacement American Republics Projects (ARP) afterwards, organized to meet this challenge and defend the integrity of the established national government. This of course included nearly all of the fairly modest *Fuerza Aérea Colombiana* (FAC), which during the intervening 60 years, must surely be counted as being amongst the most experienced in terms of anti-guerrilla operations on the planet.

Starting operations with left-over types from the Leticia period and Lend-Lease, the FAC gradually adapted more potent types to deal with the insurgency, including armed AT-6 Texans and Republic P-47D Thunderbolts, as well as an ever expanding helicopter fleet.

By the mid-1950s, the FAC was struggling to man a force that could not only meet its Rio Pact obligations as a conventional air force with national defense capabilities, with the seemingly perpetual demands of counter-insurgency, a role which inhibited the use of very capable aircraft acquired under the auspices of the Military Assistance Programs (MDAP).

This chapter remains, intentionally open ended, as the history of the FAC and its counter-insurgency operations is very much continuing, and will only be adequately chronicled when it can at last said to be over and done with.

A stalwart throughout the period of internal turmoil in Colombia, even to this day, was a large fleet of assorted Douglas C-47s. Here, FAC 650, the very first Colombian C-47A-30-DK, is seen in 1979 wearing essentially the same color scheme she had when delivered under Lend-Lease late in the Second World War. (MAP 1981-70 #269)

RIGHT: Besides mounting armament of all sorts on virtually every aircraft in the inventory to combat the guerrillas, Colombia retained quite a few of the aircraft used in the 'Leticia Incident' of the 1930s, including Junkers Ju 52/3ms. Here, FAC-625 shares the ramp with AT-6 FAC-703 and, in the distant background, four Curtiss Hawk IIs, two of them still on floats in this 1948 photograph! (Author's Collection)

ABOVE: The trio of Rawdon T-1s had a .30 caliber gun in each wing, and light bomb racks beneath the fuselage. So armed, they were obliged to fly as single-seat aircraft. (Author's Collection)

RIGHT: One of the principal elements employed by the FAC during the first, bitter period of guerrilla warfare and afterward was a sizeable fleet of Republic F-47D Thunderbolts acquired via the ARP and MDAP programs. Here, a crew pose beside a home-made napalm canister, a weapon the U.S. would not supply under MDAP. (San Diego Aerospace Musem via Fred Johnson)

ABOVE: Colombia was one of the first nations to recognize the utility of lightly armed aircraft that would later be termed COIN (Counter Insurgency) types. This led to the purchase of three rarely seen Rawdon T-1s in February 1953, serials FAC-120 to FAC-122. (Author's Collection)

19 Paraguayan Civil War   1947

Vultee BT-13A, Fuerza Aérea Gubernista, coded '65', Ñu-Guazú, Paraguay, 1947

Although emerging nominally as the victor on the ground at the conclusion of the Chaco War with Bolivia, Paraguay was exhausted on several levels, not least financially and, in human terms, from a manpower standpoint.

The result of the war was that the Military gained considerable prestige in national events, and perpetuated the fear that the Bolivians might again descend from their mountain fastness to threaten the very life of the nation. As a consequence, the country rearmed modestly

and became in all but name a reflection of the Axis temperament that was sweeping Europe by the end of the 1930s. Many Paraguayans, amongst whom German and Italian surnames were very prevalent and prominent, frankly believed during the early stages of World War Two that German and Italian arms would prevail, and the sitting regime took strength in this belief.

Allied victory, however, encouraged opposition forces, and the sitting regime was obliged to liberalize, but not fast enough nor in sufficient detail to satisfy the opposition.

By 1947, the remnants of the Chaco War era aircraft fleet had all but disappeared, and a combination of 1930s acquisitions and limited Lend-Lease supplied aircraft, totaling not more than 31 of all types, were the total assets available to the Government. These, as it turned out, became almost evenly split when factions loyal to the sitting government and the revolutionary elements chose sides and commenced hostilities against each other.

This confrontation soon took on almost operatic character, as Fairchild PT-19A primary trainers, North American AT-6Cs, Naval

Aircraft Factory N3N-3 biplanes and assorted ancillary types became ad hoc attack aircraft, carrying such weapons as they could bring to bear against each other. These included attacks against ground forces as well as against surface vessels on the main rivers, and regardless of the politics of their crews, involved enormous courage and determination in taking such fragile aircraft into harm's way.

The 1947 Paraguayan Civil War holds one particular distinction: it was almost certainly the last instance in which biplanes engaged in hostile actions in the Western Hemisphere.

ABOVE: Loyalist Fuerza Aérea Gubernista Vultee BT-13As and AT-6Cs finally responded to a number of rebel assaults. Exactly how the BT-13s were configured to carry bombs is uncertain, although some modifications to the baggage compartment were apparently involved. This is serial number '65' at Ñu-Guazú aerodrome just before the revolution with Tte. Lorenzo Alliana in the center. (via Antonio Luis Sapienza)

ABOVE: Still bearing essentially Paraguayan national markings, this Lend-Lease supplied Fairchild PT-19A was in rebel hands when photographed at Concepción in April 1947. (COL PAM René Ferreira via Antonio Luis Sapienza)

LEFT: On 17 April, one of the leaders of the rebel cause, Coronel Rafael Franco, arrived in rather modest fashion at Concepción aboard a Paraguayan Naval Aircraft Factory N3N-3 float plane, coded E-3. (via Antonio Luis Sapienza)

ABOVE: During a night reconnaissance of rebel positions on 2 July, loyalist pilot Tte.1º PAM Lorenzo Alliana was mortally wounded by ground fire, although his back-seater managed to land the aircraft and survive. Lorenzo Alliana thus gained the most unlikely honor of having been the only airman to ever be lost while piloting a PT-19 in action. (via Antonio Luis Sapienza)

One of the strangest aircraft to be involved in the revolutionary activity in Paraguay in 1947 was this Vought-Sikorsky VS-44A, bearing the Uruguayan civil registration CX-AIR. Operated nominally by an airline named TACI, it was actually used to fly arms to the rebels. (Nery Mendiburu via Antonio Luis Sapienza)

RIGHT: Pilots and crews of the so-called Arma Aérea Revolucionaria pose before the appendage of one of the Vultee BT-13As which they had seized, at their operating base at Concepción. Note the crudely painted black "V" on the fuselage, one of the few attempts to alter the markings of the rebel aircraft from those operated by the Government. (via Antonio Luis Sapienza)

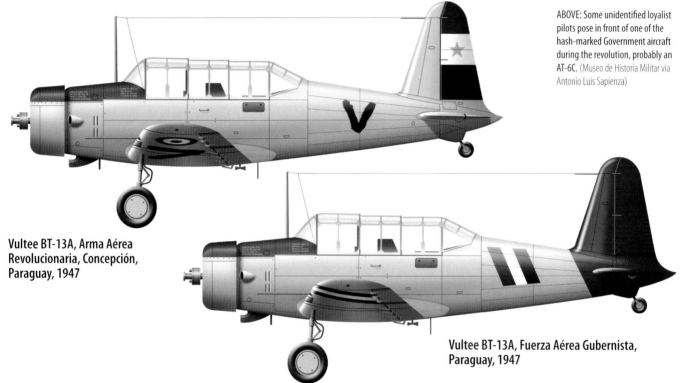

ABOVE: Some unidentified loyalist pilots pose in front of one of the hash-marked Government aircraft during the revolution, probably an AT-6C. (Museo de Historia Militar via Antonio Luis Sapienza)

Vultee BT-13A, Arma Aérea Revolucionaria, Concepción, Paraguay, 1947

Vultee BT-13A, Fuerza Aérea Gubernista, Paraguay, 1947

ABOVE: The stalwart Vultee BT-13As supplied to Paraguay under Lend-Lease during the war had no armament capability when manufactured. Both rebel and loyal forces used them in action in spite of this. Here, four BT-13As share the line with two AT-6Cs. (via Antonio Luis Sapienza)

RIGHT: As the loyalist aircraft went into action, it became clear that some means was needed to identify them against the rebel aircraft. Hence, a tri-color hash-mark was painted on the rear fuselages and outer wing panels of most aircraft, while the vertical fins and horizontal tails were painted red. (via Antonio Luis Sapienza)

20 The Caribbean Legion Period

1947 1950

Lockheed P-38L-5-VN Lightning, coded '126',
(formerly s/n 43-50310, NL-75666) Fuerza Aérea del Ejército de Cuba, 1947

This chapter is, necessarily, a summary of a number of actions involving, to one extent or another, the fabled organization which came to be known as the Caribbean Legion.

Spanning roughly the period 1946 to 1950, it is perhaps a little too easy to characterize this series of events as representing an idealistic, anti-totalitarian and anti-*Caudillo* movement aimed at toppling the well-entrenched dictatorships that seemed to ring the entire Central American, Greater Antilles and northern South American Caribbean basin.

In reality, while there certainly were men and women of high moral ideals and ideas amongst their number, the various movements inevitably became saturated with opportunists and scoundrels of a character little better and, in some instances, perhaps even worse, than the oligarchic establishments they aspired to displace.

But for the purposes of this discussion, the most striking aspect of the entire set of episodes is that the availability of relatively cheap and capable war surplus aircraft, as well as abundant numbers of out-of-work crews to crew and service them, for the first time gave opposition forces in the region what they perceived as the means to strike mortal blows to the hated dictatorships.

The first of these expeditions was the so-called Cayo Confites Affair, which had the objective of destroying the regime of Trujillo in the Dominican Republic. Well-financed and organizing a combination of ground, air and modest naval forces, this enterprise was based, with the connivance of key officials of the Cuban Government, on the remote island of Cayo Confites on Cuba's far northeast coast. The air arm of this force, which included a 'squadron' of Lockheed P-38 Lightning variants, as well as transports, medium bombardment and even one heavy bomber, gained the rather pretentious title of the *Fuerza Aérea del Ejército de la Revolucion Americana* (FAERA).

Eventually amassing some 22 aircraft of all types, this force was never tested, as Trujillo's intelligence apparatus quickly learned of the enterprise, and raised the alarm in any diplomatic venue that would hear him, and Cuba soon found herself in the awkward position of having to explain exactly how such a force came into being under the very noses of her government. In short order, the force was dispersed, the aircraft (for the most part) were absorbed into the Cuban armed forces as an unexpected bonanza, and the Legion left to bicker amongst itself as to what went wrong.

The Legion once again emerged, in name at least, in usually pacific Costa Rica in 1948, operating from the sanctuary of Guatemala, where President Juan José Arévalo hoped to use the expeditionaries in the realization of his dream of a Central American federation and coincident elimination of several specific dictatorial regimes in the neighborhood.

In March 1948, the leadership of the Legion decided to bet on an opposition group which had the objective of launching a war of national liberation in Costa Rica. Once again, aircraft figured very prominently in this episode, These included confiscated Douglas DC-3 airliners pressed into service as bombers and troop transports, three such aircraft gaining the distinction of transporting the first force of airmobile troops ever used in action in the Western Hemisphere, when 80 Legionnaires were flown into Port Limon, subsequently taking the town.

A counter-revolution ensued in Costa Rica in December 1948, prompting the newly installed, liberal government, to organized the first Costa Rican Air Force for the defense of the new regime against counter-revolutionaries operating from havens in Somoza's Nicaragua. Here, again, aircraft saw action, including some truly extraordinary examples, as described in the download text.

The final act of the Legion was yet another abortive attempt to invade the Dominican Republic in 1949, known as the Luperón Incident. Again, aircraft were the vehicle of choice, including active involvement by serving aircraft of the Guatemalan Air Force, with the blessing of President Arévalo, a very blatant example of power extension. Besides the Guatemalan C-47s, the Legion expeditionaries made use of seven aircraft, including at least two Consolidated PBY-5A Catalina amphibians, and four diverse aircraft bearing Mexican civil registrations, including a Douglas C-49E, Curtiss C-46D, Lockheed Hudson and even an Avro Anson. Of these, for various reasons, as noted in the download text, only one PBY-5A actually arrived at Luperón Bay in the Dominican Republic, after an exhausting 11 hour flight. Mistakenly expecting to find that the other elements of the invasion force had already arrived elsewhere in the country and establishing themselves, they found that a peaceful band concert was underway in Luperón. The landing party then degenerated into a tragedy of errors and, when the dust settled, the aircraft itself had been set ablaze by a Dominican Navy gun boat which arrived on the scene, and with this debacle, the so-called Caribbean Legion ended active intrigues.

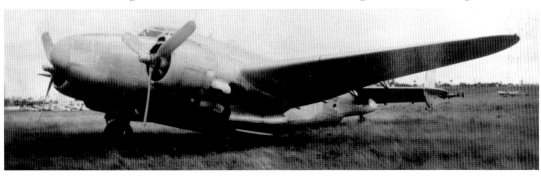

LEFT: Formerly a USAAF Lockheed B-34, this Cayo Confites aircraft appears as it was being used by the revolutionaries after seizure by Cuban authorities. It was formerly 41-38020 and RAF FD580. Just visible in the background are two P-38s, one of them in overall black. (via Leif Hellström)

RIGHT: The ill-fated Cayo Confites expedition of what was to become the Caribbean Legion amassed a small air force to support its planned invasion of Trujillo's Dominican Republic. The primary tactical aircraft were a variety of Lockheed P-38 Lightnings. CAEC 122, a P-38L-5-VN, was one of these, and is seen here after being seized by the Cubans. (via Leif Hellström)

LEFT: Another former Cayo Confites conspirator seized by the Cuerpo de Aviación, Ejercito de Cuba (CAEC) was this F-5G, serialed 123 by the Cubans. (via Leif Hellström)

Lockheed P-38L-5-VN Lightning, coded '122', (formerly s/n 43-50312, NL-5016N) Fuerza Aérea de l Ejército de Cuba, 1947

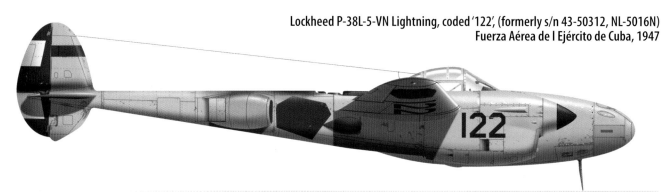

A second Lightning bound for Costa Rica, a P-38L marked "CR-02," got no further than Crane, Texas, where it ended its days in this bad landing. (Darrell Tomlinson)

LEFT/ABOVE: The solitary Consolidated PB4Y-1, bearing the code CAEC 400, was another Cayo Confites expedition aircraft. Note the pile of other Cayo Confites aircraft in the background and in the view to left which were essentially destroyed in a hurricane in October 1948. (via Leif Hellström)

**Lockheed F-5 Lightning, coded G.C.R.-01,
Fuerzas del Aire, Costa Rica, 1948**

RIGHT: Costa Rica was compelled to create a small air force in October 1948 as a direct result of the revolution in that nation which neighboring Nicaragua saw as a threat to the Somoza regime. This Lockheed F-5 Lightning, G.C.R.-01, is in the 1948 markings of that little-known air arm.
(via William T. Larkins)

The Costa Rican air arm was to have included a solitary Douglas A-24B, G.C.R.-03, but it ground-looped violently in California before departing for home. The Costa Rican 'national insignia' was an adaptation of the pre-1941 U.S. national insignia, but with the colors reversed. The disc was red, with the white star on it, with a blue central ball. (via William T. Larkins)

RIGHT: Perhaps the only post-war Douglas B-18B to see action, this was the armed Costa Rican aircraft described in the download text. It still bears remnants of its former U.S. registration, NC1037M, but was marked TI-205 with the Costa Ricans. (Emil Tkachick)

LEFT: The last gasp of the Caribbean Legion was the abortive Luperon Bay Incident of 1949. One of the key aircraft was a regular Fuerza Aérea Guatemalteca (FAG) Douglas C-47, T-1. Note the legend Ejercito de Guatemala over the fuselage insignia. (Thompson Collection)

RIGHT: Believed to have been marked only briefly in FAG markings, this Consolidated PBY-5A, FAG 50, was almost certainly the one lost at Luperon Bay, formerly NC-1096M. (LAAHS via Mario Overall)

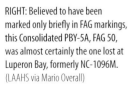

ABOVE: The Dominican defenders had a small but fairly potent array of aircraft to cope with the Luperon invasion force, had it been more successful. It included an extraordinary mix of early and late variants of the North American P-51, at the time serialed in the 400 series, as seen here. (Força Aérea magazine)

ABOVE: In addition to the P-51s, the Dominicans had a number of Lockheed P-38 and F-5 Lightnings. This F-5 has been modified to mount two .50 caliber machine guns in the nose. (Força Aérea magazine)

LEFT/LEFT BELOW: The Domincans had incorporated five De Havilland Mosquito F.B.6s and 10 Bristol Beaufighter TF.10s into their growing air arm in the fall of 1948. Although many accounts credit them as having destroyed the rebel PBY-5A at Luperon, this was not the case. (Força Aérea magazine)

BELOW: Very rarely illustrated, this is one of at least two North American P-51C Mustangs acquired by the Dominican Republic. Some of the personnel seen in this photograph were Brazilian contract pilots. (Força Aérea magazine)

21 Argentine Military and Naval Rebellion 1951

North American AT-6C, coded
'3-A-6', Escuadrilla de Ataque,
Tercera Escuadra Aeronaval,
Escuadrilla Aeronaval de Combate,
Argentina, 1951

Up to this point nearly all of Latin America had been touched, in some form, by military applications of the airplane, with the notable exception of Argentina, where, although some minor police actions had involved aircraft in support, nothing approaching the involvements elsewhere had taken place – until 1951.

The factors leading to the military and naval rebellion of September 1951 against the regime of Juan Perón are complex. Basically, as outlined in the download text, the Army and Navy, traditional guarantors of the Constitution, viewed the nomination of Perón's attractive and charismatic wife, Evita, as his Vice-President, as the last straw in a series of economic and social upheavals that had seriously eroded the military's prerogatives.

The initial aviation contribution to the revolt involved Naval AT-6 series aircraft based at Punta Indio, although little is known about their actual use. The Argentine Air Force, for the most part, remained loyal, and the leadership of the service wasted little time in launching its first-line Gloster Meteor jet fighters to intimidate the rebel Naval aviators. The Air Force also sortied a number of Avro Lincoln B.Mk.1 heavy bombers against Naval installations, and these very skilfully bombed the main Naval runway at Punta Indio, effectively neutralizing the base. One Air Force unit, however, the *Grupo 2 de Caza* based at Mendoza, and equipped with Fiat G-55A fighters for the most part, did in fact

go over to the side of the Navy. It had flown, en masse, to Punta Indio, where it was planned that they would refuel, arm and launch in support of counter-government operations. Instead, upon landing, the crews were arrested and the aircraft immobilized, as were a unit of indigenous I.Ae.-24 Calquin attack bombers that had also joined the rebel side.

News accounts of the air action during the Rebellion were lurid and often exaggerated, and as a result, this episode requires additional study by scholars of the period before the actual events, as they unfolded, can be fully understood.

ABOVE: At the time the most advanced warplane in Latin America was the Gloster Meteor F.Mk.IV used by I Escuadrón, Grupo 2 of the loyal FAA forces, to intimidate the rebel elements. C-001 was the very first Argentine Meteor. (via Dr. Gary Kuhn)

LEFT: According to one source, the only loyalist aircraft to drop bombs in anger during the 1951 rebellion were a number of Avro Lincoln B.Mk.1s of the Los Tamrindos-based Grupo I de Bombardero. The largest bombers in Latin America at the time, B-017 was typical. (British Aerospace D-356-001).

ABOVE: Besides more than 40 Fiat G-55As and G-55Bs acquired from Italy in the immediate post war years, which have been only slightly documented, Argentina also acquired one G-59 with a Rolls-Royce T.24-2 Merlin, marked C-46. It was flown by the rebel unit leader during the Rebellion, Mayor Jorge Rojas Silveira, still bearing the name Aguila.

ABOVE: The major tactical element to attempt a defection from loyalist FAA control was the Fiat G-55A equipped Escuadron of the Grupo 2 de Caza at Mendoza, along with the solitary Argentine Fiat G-59. They were grounded at the Punta del Indio NAB however, and saw no action. (via Nicholas J. Waters III).

BELOW: Perhaps the most unlikely participants in the rebellion were four elderly Northrop (Douglas) 8A-2 attack bombers that deployed briefly to Ezeiza commercial airport during the Rebellion to counter any rebel moves from there. (via Jorge Nunez Padin)

ABOVE: Another potential combatant during the Rebellion were 12 I.Aé-.24 Calquins from Los Tamarindos air base at Mendoza. The Mosquito look-alikes, like the rebel FAA Fiat G-55As and G-59, were seized by Naval personnel and grounded, however. Here, A-58 displays the unit insignia and potent armament of a service Calquin. (via Luis Santos)

22 The Bolivian Revolution   1949 1952

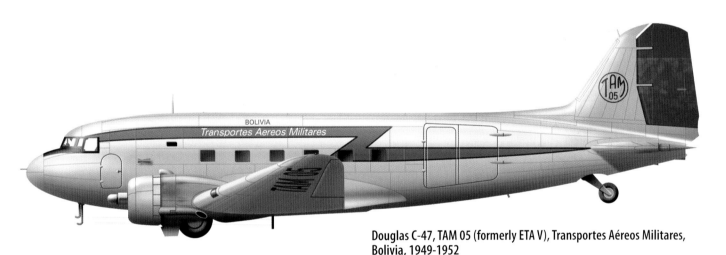

Douglas C-47, TAM 05 (formerly ETA V), Transportes Aéreos Militares, Bolivia, 1949-1952

By 1950, the traditional Bolivian ruling class had regained power and, amongst the first order of business was a purge of the armed forces to rid all branches of what were viewed as radical elements bent on social change in the remote and isolated nation.

The events that followed are almost without parallel in the modern history of any state: the regular Army and Air Force were not disbanded but, instead, were essentially ignored and allowed to wither on the vine through the nearly complete elimination of funding, and were replaced by three national militia organizations composed of miners, factory workers and *campesinos*.

Further purges, especially amongst the few talented officers and airmen remaining, followed, and the various militia groups, often acting on their own initiative, denied especially Air Force crews access to airfields, aircraft, armories, hangars and ammunition dumps.

Despite these restrictions, the Bolivian Air Force, as outlined in the download text, still managed to carry out limited operations, mainly with its fairly competent Douglas C-47 transport unit, and some limited operations by a small tactical unit equipped with North American AT-6s. A few of the C-47s were actually captured by rebel elements and pressed into service, and at least two AT-6s appear to have been lost as a result of counter-insurgency operations.

ABOVE: One of the true behind-the-scenes aircraft used by both factions during the civil war in Bolivia were variants of the sturdy Douglas C-47. At least one was lost to hostile fire. Here, C-47 TAM 05 (formerly ETA V) is surrounded by the clutter of revolution. (Henk Kavelaars Collection)

North American AT-6D Texan,
coded 'A-176', Escuadrón Tactico,
Fuerza Aérea Boliviana El Alto,
Bolivia, ca 1950

LEFT: So far as can be determined from fragmentary accounts, the only Bolivian aircraft to see tactical use during the bitter civil war period of 1949-1952 were some of the armed North American AT-6D Texans. These had the last three digits of their former U.S. serial number preceded by the letter "A". (Gnrl. Alberto Paz Soldán via Jerry Wells)

23 Operation PBSUCCESS — The CIA Backed Invasion of Guatemala — 1954

Republic F-47N Thunderbolt, coded '0568', 'Sulfato', flown by Jerry DeLarm, La Aurora, Guatemala City, 1954

By the autumn of 1953, it appeared to U.S. observers that the Guatemalan Presidency of Jacobo Arbenz Guzmán was headed towards creating a Communist state in Central America. Given the tenor of the times, with the Korean War fresh on the agenda and what seemed like world-wide Communist gains a daily occurrence, it is perhaps not surprising that the U.S., in a modern form of Gunboat Diplomacy, decided to carry out an elaborate operation to replace Arbenz with a more acceptable regime.

Often billed as the first large-scale "success" of the young Central Intelligence Agency covert operations arm, what came to be known as Operation PBSuccess was scripted to read as though written as the outline of a "B" movie.

Settling on Coronel Castillo Armas as the figurehead for its "liberation" force, the C.I.A. planners arranged for the creation of an aviation support force for his invasion of Guatemala, as described in the download text. Based on declassified C.I.A. documents, the account outlines each known mission flown by the support force during the operation, the nature and source of the aircraft involved, and their curious ultimate fates.

Likewise, for its part, the tiny Guatemalan Air Force is also detailed, together with the almost continuous effort that the Arbenz government and its agents made to supplement the air arm with efficacious aircraft before and during the short-lived conflict.

Operation PBSuccess was significant for a number of reasons. First, crucial and complete air superiority in support of the insurrection, carefully orchestrated and executed, was established – a lesson that the C.I.A. had apparently at first learned, and then quickly forgotten, by 1961. Secondly, the logistics of acquiring, manning and maintaining such a "non-traditional" air force required more than a hobbled-together assortment of "available" aircraft and skilled crews, a lesson that the C.I.A. did in fact learn as it went on to create highly effective "aviation assets" to support its mission world-wide. And finally, it taught the Agency the absolute necessity of "cleaning up" the origins of such aviation assets, in order to protect friendly persons, governments and organizations which support such activities. In retrospect, and in view of the difficulty that historians have experienced in documenting such aircraft and actions, the C.I.A., in its omnipotence, appears to have learned this lesson from the Guatemalan operation best of all.

LEFT: Although it cannot be confirmed absolutely, due to the circumstances of the transfer, this former Fuerza Aérea Hondurena (FAH) two-seat Lockheed P-38M Lightning, FAH-503, was almost certainly the aircraft used by the CIA organization during Operation PBSuccess. (Brian Baker)

BELOW: The infamous F-47N referred to as Sulfato, flown by Jerry DeLarm after the revolution at La Aurora airfield, Guatemala City. It had been one of the more active combatant aircraft in the invasion force. (via Enrique Ibarguen)

BELOW: Photographs of the CIA invasion air support force are extremely rare, for obvious reasons. The Republic F-47N Thunderbolts, all formerly Puerto Rican National Guard machines, had been completely sanitized, the solitary markings being the anti-glare panels on most (but not all) of the aircraft. The prop blades were black and had yellow hazard tips. Otherwise, the only other coloring was a black lower fuselage from the engine firewall aft. The P-38M, likewise, had only an anti-glare panel but bare metal prop blades.

BELOW: The only known photographs of the invasion force air element's Republic F-47N Thunderbolts and their unidentified ground crew. Note the P-38 Lightning in the background

RIGHT: Potentially the most serious opposition that the CIA invasion force might have encountered was in the form of three FAG Beech AT-11s fitted with bomb racks. Here, B-3, B-5, another minus its engine cowl and a Cessna UC-78 are on the line at La Aurora field. One of these was destroyed by an invasion force attack. (BG Stephen McElroy via F. A. Johnsen)

**Republic F-47N Thunderbolt, coded 'GN70',
Fuerza Aérea de Nicaragua, ca 1955**

ABOVE: Rarely illustrated, one of the Fuerza Aérea de Nicaragua (FAN) Republic F-47Ns, GN 70, after adoption of full FAN markings. Note that this example has the rarely seen blue/yellow/red roundel on the fuselage, and the more common triangular insignia on the wings. The lightning bolt insignia on the gear doors is a hold-over from PRNG use. (W. W. Martin)

ABOVE: The US Military Mission to Guatemala Douglas C-47, decoratatively marked with red/white/blue cowls, played a small part in the concluding days of Operation PBSuccess. (via Fred Johnsen)

LEFT: Another veteran of the CIA invasion force, this Douglas C-47, marked as FAG 0515, was incorporated into service after the Castillo Armas takeover. Ironically, the P-51D Mustang in the background is in Haitian markings, indicating this photo was taken at Miami. (H. G. Martin via Dr. Gary Kuhn)

24 Nicaraguan 'Invasion' of Costa Rica 1955

North American F-51D Mustang, coded '1', Fuerzas del Aire, Costa Rica, 1955

LEFT: Amongst the first aircraft to be pressed into service in the defense of the Costa Rican Government against the invasion forces from Nicaragua were Curtiss C-46D aircraft operated by the national flag carrier, LACSA, including TI-1008 shown here. The Pan American affiliation of this airline is obvious in its logo. (H. G. Martin)

LEFT: In record time, at the behest of the Organization of American States (OAS), the U.S. made available to the Costa Rican Government four North American F-51D Mustangs, flown in on 17 January from the Texas National Guard. The markings of the aircraft were expedient adaptations from the former US insignia. (Col. Dell Toedt, USAF (Ret)

Douglas C-47A, TTD-6010, Fuerza Aérea Mexicana, 1955

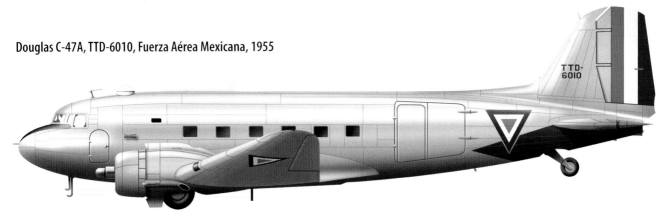

RIGHT: The OAS sent a number of aircraft from member states to supervise the disengagement of the opposing forces and to watch the invasion force from Nicaragua, including this Fuerza Aérea Mexicana (FAM) Douglas C-47A, TTD-6010. (William Haines Collection)

25 The Argentine Naval Rebellions 1955

Gloster Meteor F.Mk.IV, C-063, Tte. Ernesto Adradas, Fuerza Aérea Argentina, Base Aérea Militar (BAM) Morón, Argentina, June 1955

Juan Peron's tumultuous rule over Argentina, which had already resulted in one abortive uprising by the conservative Navy in 1951 (see Chapter 21), continued to experience ever increasing economic turbulence in his second term, heightening his difficulties and forcing him to make concessions to the industrial and commercial classes in the nation.

He was able to sustain his popular momentum by fanning a public quarrel with the Catholic Church, which fed the hostility of many senior Army and Navy officers, who were ideologically (if not spiritually) Catholic in outlook. Coupled with this, he attempted to reinsure himself against another military or naval rebellion by fostering the creation of armed union militias – a tactic seen elsewhere, with disastrous results, in Bolivia and Guatemala.

The resulting "Liberating Revolution", which was actually the work of armed factions rather than the armed forces as a whole, followed, and this time, the involvement of aircraft was significant.

The scenes that followed were little short of astonishing. In one of the first encounters, four air force Gloster Meteor F.Mk.IVs were scrambled from the base at Morón to intercept two "rebel" (Navy) North American AT-6s which were heading towards Buenos Aires. In the following, unequal match, one of the Meteors downed one of the hapless AT-6s, thus making aviation history as the first aerial victory in Latin America by a jet aircraft.

In addition to the AT-6s of a Navy attack squadron, other Naval aircraft that participated in the rebellion included a Consolidated PBY-5A, two Douglas C-47s, and a single Beech AT-11. Events transpired with lightning speed, however, and rebel elements shortly seized the air force base at Morón, where one of the Meteors, having only just returned from attacking rebel AT-6s, fell into the hands of rebel pilots, who then launched it in an attack on the government palace. Other, very determined ground missions were being carried out by Navy AT-6s based at Ezeiza against loyal Army ground units.

The confused situation was soon brought under control by forces loyal to Perón, and a number of rebels, with their aircraft, fled to nearby airfields in Uruguay, where they sought asylum.

The victory of loyal forces was short-lived, however, and in September 1955, the Navy once again took up arms against the central government. This time, the air force, bringing nearly all of its combat capable aircraft to bear, laid waste to naval air bases, although rebels did manage to gain control of at least five of the prized Meteors at Córdoba. The download text describes these actions, and the little-known series of missions carried out by a host of most unlikely aircraft.

LEFT: This Gloster Meteor F.Mk.IV, C-063, made aviation history in Latin American when, on June 16, 1955, while flown by Tte. Ernesto Adradas, it shot down a Navy North American AT-6A 3-A-23/0352, flown by Guardiamarina Arnaldo Román, who parachuted out.
(APN 144 via Ken F. Measures)

Gloster Meteor F.Mk.IV, I-079, Fábrica Militar de Aviones (FMA), Córdoba, Fuerza Aérea Argentina, as seen when seized by rebel forces in 1955

ABOVE: One of five Gloster Meteor F.Mk.IVs, I-079, seized by rebel elements of the FMA at Córdoba, and painted crudely with the distinctive insignia settled upon by at least the faction there. (Dr. Atilio Marino Collection)

ABOVE: The rebel Naval aviation element had one Consolidated PBY-5A Catalina, believed to have been 2-P-10 seen here. (via George von Roitberg)

26 The Cuban Navy Revolt 1957

Republic F-47D Thunderbolt, coded '462', Fuerza Aérea Ejercito de Cuba, Campo Columbia, Cuba, 1957

An abortive two-day revolt by elements of the Cuban Navy at the Cayo Loco naval base near Cienfuegos broke out in September 1957. Ill-fated from the start, the uprising, which was to have included both Army and Navy units, was botched from the start, and the small *Fuerza Aérea Ejercito de Cuba* (FAEC), equipped with Republic F-47D Thunderbolts and Douglas B-26 Invaders, was credited with playing a key role in defeating the movement. Interestingly, had the plot succeeded in overthrowing the sitting Batista regime and installing a new government, it might have led to unforeseen consequences for the continuing Castro insurgency in the hinterlands, and a consequent change in the course of Cuban and contemporary Caribbean history.

LEFT: The principal combat type in service with the FAEC at the time of the Naval rebellion was the Republic F-47D Thunderbolt. Here, a line-up of these still very capable aircraft are seen at Campo Columbia. (via Captain George G. Farinas)

LEFT: This rare in-flight view of FAEC F-47D 462 shows the style of national insignia in use as of the time of the Naval rebellion. Note the pirate logo on the engine cowling and the fact that the underside of the fuselage has been painted black, very common on post-war F-47s. (Marco Vidal via Omar Sixto Suarez)

ABOVE: A close-up view of the unit insignia of the Escuadron de Combate "10 de Marzo," the FAEC F-47D operating unit as of the time of the Naval rebellion. (Marco Vidal via Omar Sixto Suarez)

A very rare view of virtually the entire FAEC combat element, except the B-26s, just before the Rebellion. Note the two-color engine cowl on one of the F-47Ds and the extensive use of day-glow on the B-25J in the left background. The F-47Ds in the second row with drop tanks were MDAP aircraft enroute to Ecuador. (Col. Dell Toedt, USAF (Ret)).

Republic F-47D Thunderbolt, coded '452', Fuerza Aérea Ejercito de Cuba, Cuba, 1957

Douglas B-26C Invader, coded '931', Fuerza Aérea Ejercito de Cuba, Cuba, 1957

Border Conflict - Honduras and Nicaragua 1957

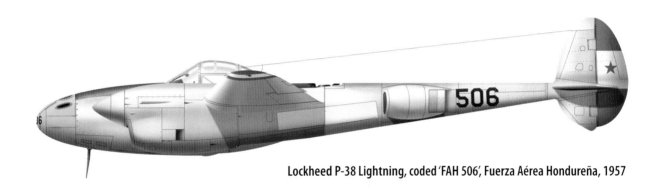

Lockheed P-38 Lightning, coded 'FAH 506', Fuerza Aérea Hondureña, 1957

In February 1957, the Honduran Government issued a decree creating a new state, to be known as Gracias a Dios, and which included territory which had been in dispute with neighboring Nicaragua for many years.

Within days, the *Fuerza Aérea Hondureña* (FAH) was ordered to ferry troops for a small garrison and supplies into the new state, using its small fleet of Douglas C-47s and commandeered civil DC-3s, escorted by Lockheed P-38 Lightnings.

Taken somewhat by surprise, the Nicaraguans reacted slowly at first, but gradually commenced patrols of the border area with a mix of aircraft, probably including North American P-51D Mustangs and T-6G Texans. Soon desultory ground attack missions were being flown in the region by both sides, although worthwhile targets were difficult to acquire and little genuine damage appears to have resulted.

Stroke and counter-stroke followed, including threats of bombing attacks on the respective national capitals, and these are described in detail in the download text.

LEFT: The Honduran combat element at the time of the adventure against Nicaragua consisted of Lockheed P-38 Lightnings and Bell P-63Es, including FAH 506. (Peter M. Bowers)

Douglas C-47, FAH-304, Fuerza Aérea Hondurena, Nicaragua, 1957

LEFT: The opening gambit of the Honduran border incursion into Nicaragua involved a mini-airlift using the entirety of the Fuerza Aérea Hondurena (FAH) Douglas C-47 transport fleet, and several commercial DC-3s, including FAH-304. (Hagedorn)

BELOW: At some point, several of the FAN P-51Ds had multi-color stripes painted on their wings and rear fuselages - possibly to aid recognition to ground forces. This is one of the very few color views of this scheme, which appears to be blue/yellow/blue/white/black. (W. W. Martin)

ABOVE: The principal aircraft available to Nicaragua to counter the Honduran border incursions were ex-Swedish North American P-51D Mustangs and armed AT-6s. Here, GN-94 undergoes maintenance in the open alongside an F-47N. (W.W. Martin via John Dienst)

Honduras very nearly brought into the action one of her rather tired-looking Consolidated PB4Y-2 Privateers, having made considerable exertions to make at least her bomb racks operational.
So far as can be determined, FAH-792 (serial just visible in small numeral on the rear fuselage) did not see action. (Peter M. Bowers)

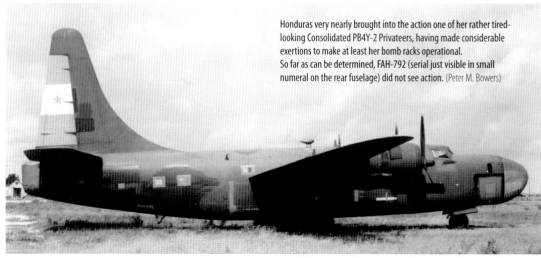

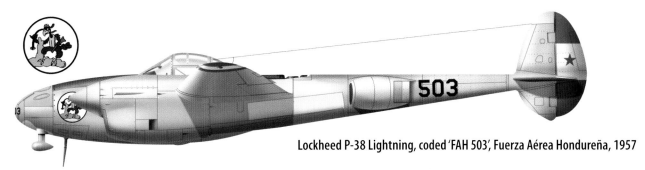

Lockheed P-38 Lightning, coded 'FAH 503', Fuerza Aérea Hondureña, 1957

LEFT: Believed to have been adopted during the border action, several of the FAH P-38s sported a form of distinctive insignia on either side of their noses, like FAH 503 shown here - almost certainly a former Operation PBSuccess P-38M. (USAF 48457AC).

28 The Venezuelan Revolution   1958

North American F-86F Sabre, coded '1B36', Escuadron de Caza Nro.36, Fuerzas Aéreas Venezolanas, Venezuela, 1958

The military dictator of Venezuela, Pérez Jiménez, often linked intimately to the similar dictatorships in the Dominican Republic and Nicaragua, finally came to grief at the hands of a left-wing military coup in January 1958, and the very well equipped *Fuerzas Aéreas Venezolanas* (FAV) played a pivotal role.

Equipped with a combination of British and U.S. jets, including de Havilland Venom F.B.4s, Vampire F.B.5s, Canberras and F-86F Sabres, it was a force to be reckoned with.

In fact, the FAV did little more than make noise and provide a highly visible show of force, although a number of the F-86Fs loyal to the sitting government did in fact attack and destroy a radio station that was supporting the rebel cause.

The download text describes the day-to-day action, and the constitution of the air forces that took part in this internecine action, and the long-term effects that they had on the evolution of air power in Venezuela.

De Havilland Venom F.B.4s of the Escuadron de Caza Nro.34, were amongst the most active of the rebel forces during the January 1958 revolt. Although taken nine years later after the adoption of newer serials, this is believed to have been one of the aircraft involved in the actions described. (Hagedorn)

BELOW: It is not clear if the Escuadron de Caza Nro.34 had adopted the name and logo of Los Indios at the time of the revolution or not. However, this is the insignia which was eventually adopted and, oddly, was carried on the center of the upper nose, rather than on the fuselage sides. (Hagedorn)

ABOVE: At the time of the 1958 action, some of the FAV aircraft had adopted the three-color "wings" to the traditional service roundel, and some had not. This March 1957 photograph shows evidence of both versions in the same setting. (USAF 105936)

LEFT: When the rebellion suddenly failed, many of the pilots who had flown for the opposition commandeered the Presidential Douglas C-54 and escaped to neighboring Colombia. Serialed 7AT1, the aircraft has since been returned to Venezuela and is now on display at the FAV museum at Maracay. (Hagedorn)

Aircraft which remained loyal to the Government included the North American F-86F Sabres of the Escuadron de Caza Nro.36, which actually fired their guns and underwing rockets in anger. (H. G. Martin)

29 Bay of Pigs - The Air War   1961

Douglas B-26B Invader in markings of a 'defecting' machine of the Fuerza Aérea Revolucionaria, coded 'FAR-933', Miami, 15 April 1961

Although much has been written about the disastrous C.I.A. attempt to topple the Castro regime via an invasion in 1961, little space has been devoted to detailing the crucial role of aviation in the events as they unfolded.

This chapter examines, in detail, the conception, training, organization and execution of the aviation support, as well as the claims and counter-claims that have made by both sides ever since.

Although the aircraft involved have been fairly accurately portrayed in most accounts, several historical anomalies have escaped detailed discussion. For example, perhaps the ultimate flaw in the entire operation was the decision to curtail the highly detailed plan to destroy Castro's existing air assets prior to actually landing the invasion force. In retrospect, this decision, coupled with the apparently unexpected competence of the surviving Castro aircrews in handling and engaging their remaining aircraft, doomed the enterprise and resulted in tragic fates for most of the invaders and a stinging – and long-lasting – blow to U.S. pride and national image.

That the entire operation could have been salvaged at a number of key junctures, or at least given a better chance of achieving some limited goals, seems clear. That the failure of the U.S. leadership to make good military decisions sealed the fate of the operation is equally clear.

Politics and generalship aside, the aircraft and crews involved have acquired an almost legendary status, and the heroism and airmanship of all concerned, given the circumstances and stakes, must rank this episode as one of the most significant aerial encounters of the first 100 years of manned flight in Latin America.

ABOVE: The infamous Douglas B-26B marked as FAR-933, which embarrassed U.S. ambassador to the U.N., Adlai Stevenson when it supposedly 'defected' from Cuba. It was, course, a Brigada 2506 diversion and part of the overall plan for the start of the hoped for uprising against Castro. (Avance)

THIS PAGE: Photographed derelict in the area of Miami International Airport formerly known as "corrosion corner," this abandoned Douglas B-26B Invader (built as A-26C 43-22729), marked only as N9424Z, was one of the earliest participants in the clandestine war against Fidel Castro. It was last registered to Richard H. Steves and F.A. Conner in 1963. (Javier Quintero)

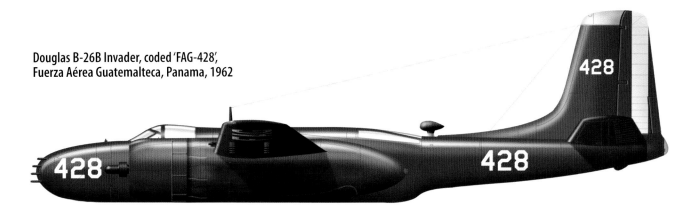

Douglas B-26B Invader, coded 'FAG-428',
Fuerza Aérea Guatemalteca, Panama, 1962

ABOVE: The mix of Douglas B-26 Invaders provided to the Fuerza Aérea Guatemalteca (FAG) under MAP were, for a time, operated by invasion force crews for training in full Guatemalan markings. FAG-420 was one of these. (via Edward Ferrer)

LEFT/BELOW: There is considerable evidence that the eight B-26s provided to the FAG and which were shared with the CIA invasion force crews for training were, at least in part, replaced after losses by others. Here, FAG-428, clearly painted in black intruder color scheme, undergoes main spar rehabilitation in Panama in 1962. (Peter Fletcher) In the second view , FAG-428 shows only a short time later, black on the engine cowl flaps. (Enrique Ibarguen)

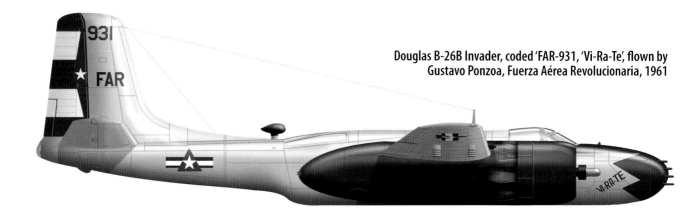

Douglas B-26B Invader, coded 'FAR-931', 'Vi-Ra-Te', flown by
Gustavo Ponzoa, Fuerza Aérea Revolucionaria, 1961

LEFT: Before the actual attack, at
least some of the invasion force
B-26s received 'noseart' and special
markings, including this aircraft,
Vi-Ra-Te, flown by Gustavo Ponzoa
from Happy Valley.

(Gustavo Ponzao via Leif Hellström)

ABOVE: Some of the B-26s used
late in the invasion attempt were
scrubbed clean of all markings
except blue bands around the wings
just outboard of the rocket rails, to
avoid further confusion with the
'genuine' FAR B-26s.

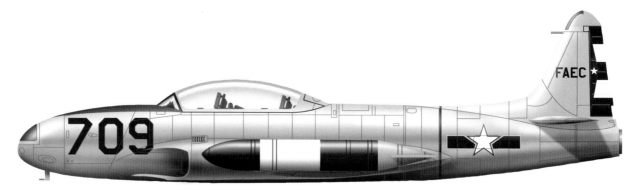

Lockheed T-33A, coded '709', Fuerza Aérea Ejercito de Cuba, Cuba, ca 1956-57

LEFT: One of the pivotal aircraft in
the failure of the invasion attempt
was the Lockheed T-33As which had
been provided to the pre-Castro
FAEC under MDAP. Here, FAEC-709
bears the full color scheme used
until Castro seized power.

(via Captain George G. Farinas)

LEFT/BELOW: Of nearly equal importance to Castro's defeat of the invasion force were the remaining airworthy Hawker Sea Fury F.B.11s. Initially, these were natural metal/doped aluminum with Cuban markings. (Javier Quintero)

LEFT: Cuba also acquired two of the two-seat trainer versions of the Sea Fury, T.Mk.20s. These were armed with rocket rails and guns, and at least one was painted in the so-called "Cuban olive drab" color scheme. (via Captain George G. Farinas)

Hawker Sea Fury F.B.11, coded '505', Fuerza Aérea Ejercito de Cuba, Cuba,1958

Hawker Sea Fury T.Mk.20, coded '575', Fuerza Aérea Ejercito de Cuba, Cuba,1958

ABOVE: This Cuban Sea Fury F.B.11, FAR-541, is purported to be wearing the color scheme "Cuban olive drab" and armament combination used to combat the invasion force. This has escaped verification. (via George von Roitberg)

ABOVE: It is virtually certain that most, if not all, of the Cuban Sea Furies had been painted over-all "Cuban olive drab" by the time of the invasion. Here, serial 530 bears such a scheme, with rocket rails in place and a C-46 in the background. (via Captain George G. Farinas)

30 Guatemalan Counter-Insurgency   1962 1992

Douglas C-47, coded 'FAG-540', Fuerza Aérea Guatemalteca, Guatemala, 1979

Although overshadowed by the later Sandinista and Contra insurgency in Central America, and the so-called Salvadorian "civil war", the nearly 30-year internal struggles endured in nearby Guatemala witnessed the first practical, and nearly surgical, application of what came to be known as "Counter-Insurgency" (COIN) aviation anywhere.

Conducted on what appeared to some observers to be a rather casual basis, the *Fuerza Aérea Guatemalteca* (FAG) and its personnel, which in conjunction with selected and highly-trained Guatemalan Army units bore the brunt of the action, in some instances never knew anything but such low-intensity warfare during their entire career with the service. The experience in close-support operations thus gained, first with a small fleet of North American F-51D Mustangs and assorted support aircraft, and later with Cessna A-37B light attack jets, must have been amongst the most intensive anywhere. At the same time, the crews must also have become jaded to the powerful effects of their weapons and, perhaps, less careful in their application, with consequent implications for innocent victims and public opinion in the remote, guerrilla-infested regions of the country.

Although the service gradually adopted rotary-wing aircraft to support Army units in the field against the insurgents as the struggle evolved, it was only with the most daunting of logistics challenges, as the human rights issues which inevitably surfaced resulted in a virtual world-wide embargo on arms support to the central government. The FAG, as a direct consequence, was reduced to subterfuge and intrigue to acquire even the most rudimentary spares, and was obliged for a time to paint their aircraft with civilian paint schemes and civil registrations to cloak their actual mission.

It may be years before the full extent of FAG operations - and losses – during this 30 year period are fully understood, but he download text of this chapter lays down the framework for additional research.

ABOVE: One of the last known photographs of F-51Ds in Guatemala, this curious air show image shows the past, present and future in a scene which must surely be calculated to ruin a safety officers' day! The oldest airworthy Waco VPF-7, a new Cessna A-37B, and at least three camouflaged Mustangs are seen here at La Aurora field. (Mario Overall)

Lockheed T-33A, coded '721', Escuadron de Ataque y Reconocimiento (SAW), Fuerza Aérea Guatemalteca, Guatemala, January 1970

ABOVE: The two principle tactical aircraft types included on the strength of the FAG's Escuadron de Ataque y Reconocimiento (SAW) by 1968 were Lockheed T-33As and North American F-51D Mustangs. This lineup of five, represent virtually all of the airworthy examples at the time, as shown here in January 1970, by which time they had been organized into an ad hoc aerial demonstration team
(Hagedorn)

RIGHT: The Guatemalan T-33s consisted of both T-33A-1-LOs and AT-33A-20-LO, both capable of delivering ordnance. This is T-33A-1-LO FAG-721, showing details of the exotic color scheme of January 1970.
(Hagedorn)

BELOW: By far the most numerous aircraft the FAG began to use were the North American F-51D Mustangs from July 1954. During the course of almost all the 30 years that followed, the variety of color schemes worn by these aircraft was little short of amazing. Nearly all of them were engaged in the COIN actions at some time or another. This is probably FAG-315.
(Dave Henry via Leif Hellström)

LEFT: With other FAG aircraft of the counter-guerrilla era in the background, including C-47s (complete with day glow) 520 and 530, a gray and a black B-26 and a Cessna 170, this F-51D shows evidence of having fired the two in-board guns.
(Dave Henry via Leif Hellström)

LEFT/ABOVE: By December 1966, most of the surviving FAG F-51s had been painted a light-gray overall, but with some individual markings, as on the prop spinner of FAG-357 seen here. The FAG also operated at least one rare, genuine TF-51D during this period, FAG-349 seen here on line. (both Bob MacArthur)

North American F-51D Mustang, coded 'FAG-357', Fuerza Aérea Guatemalteca, Guatemala, December 1966

LEFT: U.S. Military Assistance Program planners attempted to expand the COIN capabilities of the FAG by supply of some Sikorsky UH-19s, at least one of which was later armed with door and ski-mounted weapons. This is FAG-130 as it appeared in December 1967. (Tom Surlak)

ABOVE: Guatemala acquired a variety of Cessna 170 and 180 aircraft from commercial sources and MAP. FAG-672 and the oddly camouflaged example behind it, are believed to have been the rarely seen Cessna U-17Cs. (Tom Surlak)

RIGHT: Five FAG Douglas C-47s, five F-51Ds and two T-33As - one with a white band around the rear fuselage - share the ramp at La Aurora field as of December 1967. (Tom Surlak).

Douglas C-47, coded 'FAG-520', 'Juracán', Fuerza Aérea Guatemalteca, Guatemala, December 1966

RIGHT: Also vital to the movement of troops to combat the guerrilla attacks were the small transport element of the FAG, which operated mainly Douglas C-47 variants. FAG-520 bears the name Juracán and an unknown emblem on her nose in this December 1966 view.
(Hagedorn)

LEFT: By 1979, deep into the guerrilla war, the bright white-upper color schemes and day glow of the 1960s had given way to the far more practical random camouflage schemes adopted by the service at that time. FAG-540 should have been the eighth C-47 acquired by the service.
(Norm Taylor via John Kerr).

RIGHT: Ostensibly the 'first' Guatemalan Douglas C-47, FAG-500, shares the La Aurora ramp in December 1967 with the much 'younger' FAG-525. The Guatemalans numbered their C-47s in increments of five digits at the time, suggesting that this last example was the sixth C-47 acquired since this convention started.
(Tom Surlak)

RIGHT: A variation on the color scheme of '315' below, this quartet of FAG F-51Ds all have completely different camouflage schemes, but appear to have a Guatemalan flag on the vertical fins. (FAG via Bob Dorr)

BELOW: The same aircraft pictured earlier in bare metal on page 151. Here is FAG-315 again with yet another variation on the guerrilla era camouflage scheme. (via John Dienst)

ABOVE: Believed to have been the final four airworthy, anti-guerrilla FAG F-51Ds, these aircraft appear as they arrived in the U.S. after being sold as surplus. Contrary to some reports, the unusual crests seen on two of the aircraft were of Guatemalan origin. (via John Dienst)

BELOW: In May 1971, the FAG received the first of at least 14 Cessna A-37B light attack jets. These nimble aircraft soon brought use of the F-51D to an end, as spares shortages and wear-and-tear took its toll, and they assumed the bulk of the COIN operations. (via Nicholas J. Waters III)

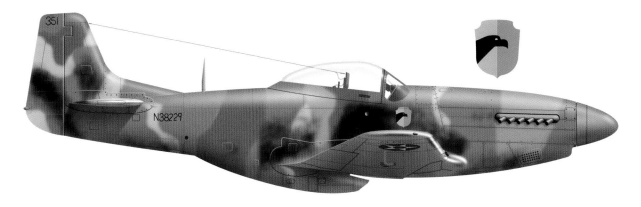

North American F-51D Mustang, believed to be coded 'FAG-351', Fuerza Aérea Guatemalteca, Guatemala, ca 1970-72

31 The Invasion of Haiti

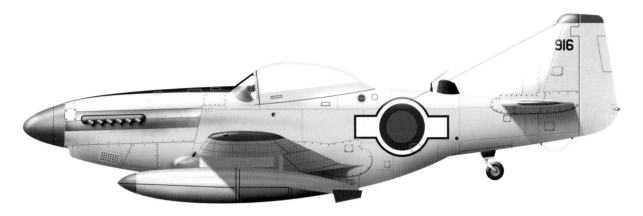

North American F-51D Mustang, s/n 916, Corps d'Aviation d'Haiti, Republic of Haiti, ca 1963

Perhaps nowhere in Latin America is the poverty and social privation of the average person more primitive than on the western half of the island of Hispaniola, known as the Republic of Haiti.

Dominated for much of its modern existence by absolute dictatorships, it is hard to conceive that, in spite of everything, opposition groups managed to emerge, organize, and even mount modest attempts at toppling the medieval regimes that persisted.

What is perhaps even more surprising is that these expeditions often included an aviation component, as reaching the island by almost any other means was difficult at best.

The download text describes these abortive expeditions, and the array of aircraft that the regime supported, in a rather curious way, to oppose them.

LEFT/ABOVE: The only tactical aircraft of any importance to the besieged dictatorships of Haiti during the several abortive invasion attempts were small batches of North American P-51D and F-51D Mustangs acquired from May 1951. This aircraft, serial 916, almost certainly the former N103TL, was one of the last two acquired, flown to Haiti clandestinely. The drop tanks are allegedly from an F-86. (via Luis Santos)

32 Argentine Revolution 1963

Vought F4U-5NL Corsair, coded '3-A-204', Argentine Aeronaval, Argentina, 1963

The Argentine armed forces were once again involved in internal politics in September 1962 – the fifth time in 13 months – leading to the so-called "revolution of the Reds and Blues" of 2-4 April zh1963.

Although once again mired in internal politics, stroke and counter-stroke, Naval aviation units, after their stinging decimation of 1955 (see Chapter 24), had survived and, in fact, been revitalized, and soon found itself once again being pitted against regular Army and Air Force units, while the general populace largely ignored the proceedings.

From the very beginning, however, the revolt went badly, in what was very nearly a comic-opera set of misadventures. Loyal Army and *Fuerza Aérea Argentina* (FAA) units managed to route a force of Argentine Marines, driving them from the capital, although Navy Grumman F9F-2 Panther jet fighter bombers and Vought F4U-5NL Corsairs, combined with armed North American AT-6s, managed to inflict considerable damage on an Army armored force. This attack, however, did little more than provoke the FAA into attacking the Navy airbase at Punta Indio, where, once again, a significant number of Naval aircraft were destroyed on the ground.

This affair was significant in that it was the first instance in which jet fighters potentially faced other jet fighters in Latin American aviation history, although the Navy's F9F-2s and the FAA's F-86Fs apparently never actually encountered one another in flight during the revolt.

ABOVE: The pride of the Comando de Aviación Naval (CAN), and the first (and, until recently, only) Naval jets in Latin America, six of the 24 acquired Argentine Grumman F9F-2 Panthers share the line here with two Grumman F9F-8T Cougars.
(via Jorge Nunez Padin)

LEFT: The Navy lost heavily in the 1963 revolt. The nearest F9F-2 Panther seen here, 3-A-118, was amongst at least seven completely destroyed by loyal air attacks.
(via George G. J. Kamp)

ABOVE: Flying over the Argentine aircraft carrier, F9F-2 Panther 3-A-106 trails smoke during happier times. This aircraft survived the 1963 revolt and served on until deactivation in 1971.
(via Carlos A. Eraso)

RIGHT: The Argentine Navy employed a number of veteran Vought F4U-5NL Corsairs against loyal Army armored units during the 1963 revolt.
(Carlos Alberto Eraso)

North American F-86F Sabre, coded 'C-101', Fuerza Aérea Argentina, Argentina, ca 1963

The loyal Fuerza Aérea Argentine (FAA), flying some of its relatively new North American F-86F Sabres, inflicted considerable damage on the naval aviation units at Punta del Indio NAB. C-101 was the first FAA F-86F, delivered in September 1960, but was written off in an accident in May 1968. (Marcelo W. Miranda)

33 Intervention - Dominican Republic 1965

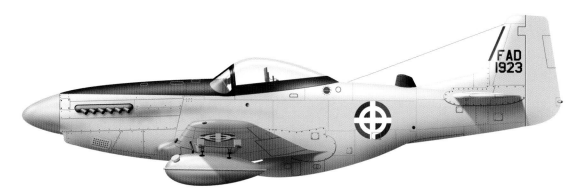

North American P-51D Mustang, coded 'FAD-1923', Fuerza Aérea Dominicana, Dominican Republic, 1965

On April 24, 1965, followers of ousted President Juan Bosch rose up in arms in the Dominican Republic against the central government, resulting in the commander of the *Fuerza Aérea Dominicana* (FAD) launching heavily armed and recently refurbished North American P-51D Mustangs against suspected rebel positions throughout the capital.

The existing junta requested Organization of American States (OAS) action to help restore order and, commencing 29 April, U.S. and, later, contingents from a number of other Latin American nations, arrived to separate the combatants and resolve the internal strife.

BELOW: By 1965, the once-mighty Fuerza Aérea Dominicana (FAD) of the Trujillo era was but a shadow of its former glory. The best surviving ex-Swedish North American P-51D Mustangs had been radically overhauled in Florida by Trans-Florida Aviation, and a number of these attempted to quell the internal trouble that led to OAS intervention. (via Roger Besecker)

RIGHT: When OAS forces arrived, including major elements of the U.S. 82nd Airborne Division, one of their first measures was to essentially arrest the marauding FAD P-51Ds, which had been attacking targets in the country almost indiscriminately. (USAF 101202).

BELOW: Although at least 10 ex-Swedish De Havilland Vampires, several Douglas B-26 Invaders, and at least two North American B-25 Mitchells were intact and nominally airworthy at the time of the 1965 civil war, none are known to have taken any role in the action. (Garry R. Pape)

34 Che Guevara in Bolivia

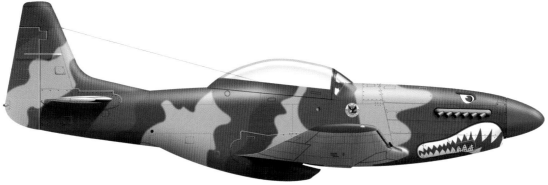

Cavalier TF-51D Mustang, Grupo Aéreo de Caza, Fuerza Aérea Boliviana, Bolivia, 1967

The death of the almost legendary Cuban insurgent, Ernesto "Che" Guevara, in a remote region of Bolivia in 1967 led subsequently to what has amounted to an unbelievable avalanche of speculation and near mystification as to the circumstances of his defeat there.

In fact, although his demise was largely due to a complete lack of acceptance by the average Bolivian *campesino*, his band of revolutionaries was hounded almost continuously by the small but well-trained counter-insurgency force of the *Fuerza Aérea Boliviana* (FAB).

This chapter surveys the organization and equipment of the FAB, and the hitherto little-known role that the service played in the defeat of this ill-advised expedition.

ABOVE: Besides batches of MAP-supplied Cessna U-17s, most of the pressure brought to bear against the Guevara band came at the hands of the Fuerza Aérea Boliviana's (FAB) veteran North American P-51D Mustangs. Here, FAB-511 displays the feisty tiger-mouth markings believed to have been adopted during the action. (DIA)

ABOVE: The U.S. rushed a batch of Cavalier-rebuilt F-51D Mustangs to the FAB to aid in the campaign against the Guevara band, but they arrived late in the episode and, so far as can be determined, probably only took part in the mop up operations. These aircraft initially wore both their U.S. fiscal year serial and FAB serials. (DIA)

RIGHT: As the FAB integrated the new Cavalier F-51Ds into its primary tactical unit, the bright pre-Guevara schemes gave way to Vietnam-era camouflage. This Cavalier TF-51D bears unit insignia and tiger-mouth only, with no sign of serial number or national insignia. (Hagedorn)

Cavalier TF-51D Mustang, coded 'FAB 522' Grupo Aéreo de Caza, Fuerza Aérea Boliviana, Bolivia, 1967

LEFT: The Mustangs employed against the Guevara band were operated at the time by the Grupo Aéreo de Caza, the distinctive insignia of which is seen reproduced faithfully on one of the P-51s that returned later to the U.S.
(Eden Harriss via John Dienst)

ABOVE: When received under MAP, the Cavalier-rebuilt F-51Ds and TF-51Ds were truly beautiful aircraft, and the FAB wasted no time painting tiger-mouths on them.
(FAB)

34 "El Guerra de 100 Horas" 1969

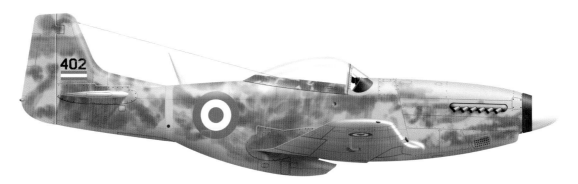

Cavalier F-51D Mustang, coded '402', Fuerza Aérea Salvadoreña, El Salvador, 1969

It is appropriate that this work should conclude with the so-called "Soccer War", of rather short duration, which erupted between neighboring Honduras and El Salvador in 1969.

It is significant for a number of reasons. First and foremost, it witnessed what was almost certainly the final air-to-air combat between conventional, piston-engined aircraft in the history of aviation, and thus signaled the end of an era. Second, it served as a nearly text-book example of how even small nation states could muster credible aerial forces to achieve political and social objectives.

For the first time, a detailed analysis of all known missions is presented, and a number of long-standing myths are examined and debunked. Although seemingly evenly matched on paper, in fact the Hondurans enjoyed one advantage that Salvador could not: depth of terrain in which to shield and marshal her forces.

The war also saw the use of most unlikely aircraft as combatants, with Douglas C-47 transports being employed by both sides as bombers, and a sizeable contribution made on the Salvadoran side by what amounted to lightly armed civilian aircraft flown by volunteers in light reconnaissance missions. That the Hondurans did not encounter and destroy these intruders is due only to the fact that the density of aircraft which they could muster and scramble at any one time was actually rather low.

As in most other conflicts in Latin America involving neighboring states, the 1969 war resulted in an arms race between Honduras and Salvador which, stimulated by the Contra period that followed, resulted in each nation acquiring aircraft in numbers that would have been unheard-of under any other circumstances.

RIGHT: One of the opening moves in the brief 1969 war between El Salvador and Honduras came in a most unusual form - an FAS Douglas C-47 converted to a make-shift bomber. FAS-101 was a veteran aircraft, and very probably was still marked like this when the war started. Note the wingtip of the similarly painted FG-1D, FAS-220, to the right.
(BG Hal Ahrens via Dave Ostrowski)

Douglas C-47, s/n 103, Fuerza Aérea Salvadoreña, El Salvador, 1969

ABOVE: Although the FAS had acquired 20 surplus Goodyear-built FG-1D Corsairs in 1957, not all of them received the special air show color scheme worn here by FAS-215. This scheme was gone before the 1969 war on all but derelict examples.
(BG Hal Ahrens via Dave Ostrowski)

RIGHT: Nearly complete air-show color scheme as worn by FG-1D FAS-220 until just before the 1969 war. This particular aircraft survived to be the last FAS Corsair, being sold back to the U.S. in April 1989.

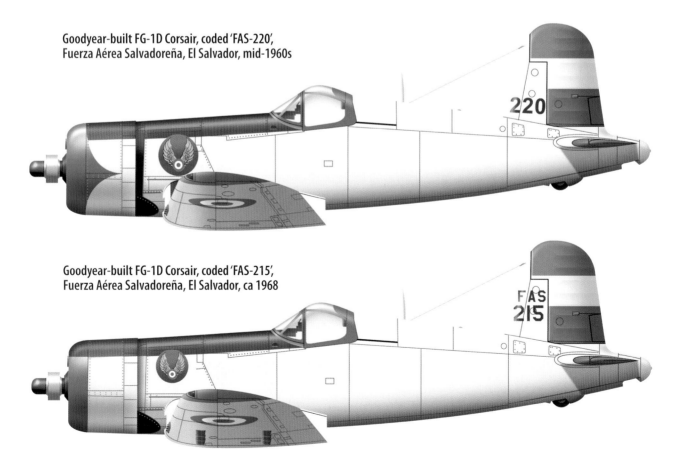

Goodyear-built FG-1D Corsair, coded 'FAS-220',
Fuerza Aérea Salvadoreña, El Salvador, mid-1960s

Goodyear-built FG-1D Corsair, coded 'FAS-215',
Fuerza Aérea Salvadoreña, El Salvador, ca 1968

ABOVE/LEFT/TOP: Contrary to popular belief, not all FAS Corsairs were gaily painted. Here, FAS-207, FAS-208 and FAS-218 clearly show that the former U.S. Navy dark blue was retained on a number of the aircraft, with the simple addition of white FAS logo, serials and some additional markings in certain cases. (Archie Baldocchi)

FG-1D Corsair, coded 'FAS-207', Fuerza Aérea Salvadoreña, El Salvador

LEFT: Neighboring Honduras, which was attacked by El Salvador, was also employing variants of the Corsair as first-line equipment, although the Fuerza Aérea Hondurena (FAH) examples were a mix of F4U-4s and F4U-5Ns. Here, F4U-5s, FAH-601 and -604, show the considerable wear and tear that these veteran aircraft, acquired in 1956, had attained by 1969. (COL Bassett via Carlos Planas)

BOTTOM OF PAGE: Although bearing a small U.S. civil registration for her trip back to the U.S., Honduran F4U-4 FAH-612 looks almost exactly as she did during the 100 Hour War. Note that she has one of 609s drop tanks, however! (LTV via Jay Miller)

F4U-5 Corsair, coded 'FAH-601', Fuerza Aérea Hondurena, Honduras, mid-1960s

FAR LEFT: From left to right, Sub-Tte. Leopoldo Suarez, Cpt. Guillermo Reynaldo Cortez and mechanic Cuco Sanchez pose before a camouflaged FG-1D at the secret Salvadoran deployment airstrip at La Libertad, San Andres 16 July 1969. (Cpt. Douglas Cornejo)

LEF/BELOW: Within a short time of the start of hostilities, the need for special markings to distinguish friend from foe became apparent. The airworthy FAS FG-1Ds soon sported yellow identification bands around the engine cowl, rear fuselage, and the wings, in the region of the gun apertures. (Guido E. Buehlmann)

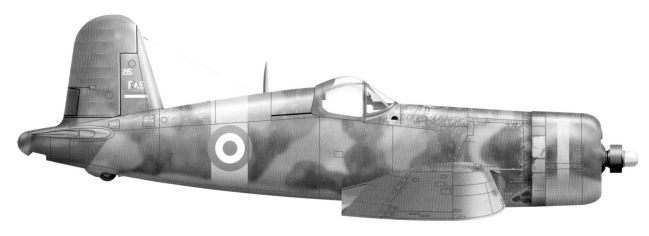

FG-1D Corsair, coded 'FAS-215', Fuerza Aérea Salvadoreña, El Salvador, 1969

RIGHT: The final six surviving Honduran Corsairs, a mix of F4U-4s and F4U-5Ns, shortly after their return to the U.S. - all combat veterans. (LTV via Jay Miller)

LEFT : The Hondurans, while surprised by the Salvadoran attack, soon organized their considerable forces to combat the invasion. This aircraft, F4U-5N FAH-609, later to become famous as the mount of Mayor Fernando Soto, is seen here named 'Snap Shot'. It is fully loaded with 20 mm guns, a drop tank to starboard and a 250-pound bomb to port, and eight rockets. (via Carlos Planas)

ABOVE: No clear record has been found detailing the nicknames or noseart carried by the Honduran Corsairs. Here, FAH-606, an F4U-5N, is named 'Tarranas', and is having its guns loaded. (via Carlos Planas)

F4U-5N Corsair, coded 'FAH-606', 'Tarranas', Fuerza Aérea Hondurena, Honduras, 1969

Besides the F4U-5Ns received earlier, Honduras also acquired a batch of F4U-4s, including FAH-614. They saw action during the war in roughly equal numbers. (COL Bassett via Carlos Planas)

Arguably the most historic aircraft of the conflict, F4U-5N FAH-609 shortly after the end of the war, complete with Mayor Soto's victory markings for two FAS FG-1Ds and a Mustang. This aircraft survives, and will become the centerpiece of a new museum. (Carlos Planas)

F4U-5N Corsair, coded 'FAH-609' flown by Mayor Fernando Soto Enriquez, Fuerza Aérea Hondurena, Honduras, 1969

LEFT: The Honduran crews had considerable experience on their aircraft, and generally committed themselves very well during the conflict. This frontal view of F4U-4 FAH-615 is in front of the distinctive Cuartel Mayor at Tegucigalpa's Toncontin airfield, a frequent target of Salvadoran raiders.
(LTV via Jay Miller)

LEFT: The Hondurans flew a number of operational missions with this Douglas C-54, FAH-798, during the war which would today be cited as AWACS missions. (Hagedorn)

RIGHT: Honduras also had a handful of North American T-28 Trojans which took a limited part in the hostilities. They were capable of mounting ordnance on a single pylon under each wing. This is EAM-213, photographed in March 1976. (Carlos Planas)

Lockheed T-33A, coded 'FAH-222', Fuerza Aérea Hondurena, Honduras, ca 1969

LEFT: Something of a mystery aircraft, it is not clear at the time of writing whether Honduras had acquired a single Lockheed T-33A before, during, or after the conflict. While some reports cite high-speed reconnaissance flights by this aircraft, subsequent accounts state that FAH-222 was not acquired until after the war was over. (COL Bassett via Carlos Planas)

RIGHT: FAS and Salvadoran civil light aircraft flew a significant number of missions in support of the ground offensive. This Cessna U-17A was amongst these. (Fred Young)

LEFT: One of the most potent weapons in the Salvadoran arsenal were the small batch of Cavalier F-51D Mustang IIs that had been acquired in late 1967 and 1968. Here, FAS-405 undergoes maintenance in the field while still sporting her wing-tip tanks, which were soon to be deleted. (Archie Baldocchi)

ABOVE: Another of the Cavalier Mustang IIs, FAS-403 reveals that, after the wing-tip tanks were deleted, the tips were painted flat black but the white service logo was retained on the upper starboard wing. (Archie Baldocchi)

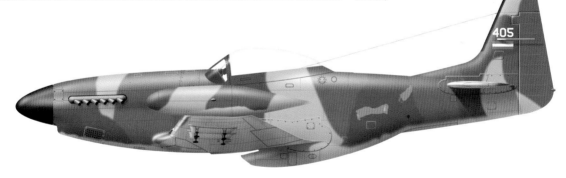

Cavalier F-51D Mustang II, coded 'FAS-405', Fuerza Aérea Salvadoreña, El Salvador, 1969

Another view of Cavalier Mustang II taken only slightly later, now without wing tip tanks, and showing evidence of combat repair damage to the mid fuselage. (Archie Baldocchi)

LEFT/ABOVE LEFT: Maintenance on the FAS tactical fleet was carried out at remote deployment airstrips with the crudest of facilities throughout the conflict. This Cavalier F-51, FAS-405, seems to be receiving considerable attention. This view shows the rather odd position of the small Salvadoran roundel on the upper port wing.
(Archie Baldocchi)

ABOVE: Within days of the opening of hostilities, the Cavalier F-51s had their wing-tip tanks removed and narrow yellow identification bands added to the rear fuselage and wings outboard of the guns. Here, FAS-405 and 403 share the ramp with a Cessna U-17A and a C-47 at Ilopango. (Archie Baldocchi)

ABOVE: Quickly realizing that the FAH was no longer a paper tiger, Salvador frantically cast around for additional stock P-51 Mustangs to supplement her combat element. These soon began to arrive, and every one was painted individually according to the taste of the crews who worked on them. This is one of these aircraft on its first operational mission, in the hands of Bob Love, over La Union. (Archie Baldocchi)

RIGHT: An extremely rare air-to-air photograph of an FAS Cavalier Mustang II, FAS-405, on patrol during the war. Note that on the camera plane, the white FAS titles on the upper starboard wing had been partly overpainted by the yellow identification band.
(Archie Baldocchi)

LEFT: At some point, the serial number on FAS-405 was shortened to just 05 and a prominent Salvadoran roundel added to the fuselage. (Archie Baldocchi)

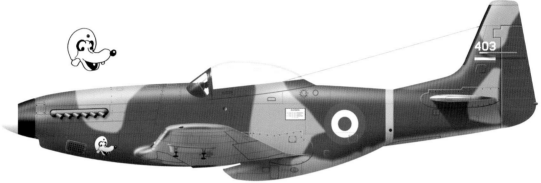

Cavalier F-51D Mustang II, 'FAS-03', Fuerza Aérea Salvadoreña, El Salvador, early 1970s

ABOVE: Salvador's Cavalier Mustangs served until September 1975, when the surviving examples were sold to private U.S. owners. Here, FAS-403 is seen in a 1971 post-war pose, with a white prop spinner cap and the Lobo insignia on the lower engine cowl. This aircraft crashed in 1974. (via Marco Antonio Lavagnino)

RIGHT: Another view of Cavalier Mustang II FAS-403 which shows the wrap-around camouflage scheme on the leading edges of the wings and the very small diameter Salvadoran national insignia on the lower starboard wing. (Archie Baldocchi)

FAS-407 appears to have had her lower engine cowling painted differently - or was taken from another aircraft. Note the P-51 in the background with a yellow prop spinner and completely different camouflage scheme. (Archie Baldocchi).

THIS SPREAD/OVERLEAF: There was no attempt at standardization in the colors of the stock P-51Ds acquired by Salvador.

North American F-51D Mustang, 'coded FAS-407', Fuerza Aérea Salvadoreña, El Salvador, early 1970s

ABOVE: FAS-406 has a black prop spinner and full combat markings. (Guido E. Buehlmann).

Aanother variation on the theme, FAS-409 retains the upper rear fuselage blade antenna of her former U.S. civil owner.
(Archie Baldocchi).

North American F-51D Mustang, 'coded FAS-406', Fuerza Aérea Salvadoreña, El Salvador, early 1970s

LEFT: This aircraft had a white prop spinner by 1974, and the officer on the wing was the (then) FAS CO, Mayor Regalado. The badge on the fuselage is a screaming chimpanzee, thus the nickname of this aircraft, 'El Mono', which was also the nickname of the pilot, Otto Vega Monofelo.
(Marco Antonio Lavagnino).

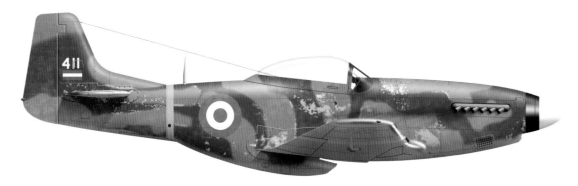

North American F-51D Mustang, 'coded FAS-411', Cpt. Avila Rosales, Fuerza Aérea Salvadoreña, El Salvador, 1969

LEFT: A historic photograph. FAS-411 was almost certainly the last Mustang lost in action in any war, when Cpt. Avila Rosales was downed at Amatecampo. The circumstances of his loss are unknown.
(Marco A. Lavagnino)

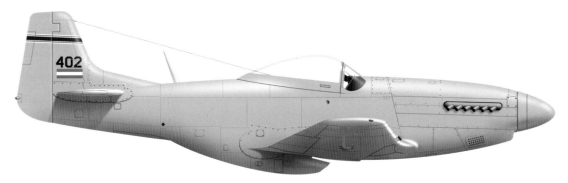

North American P-51D Mustang, coded 'FAS-402', Fuerza Aérea Salvadoreña, El Salvador, 1969

ABOVE/RIGHT: Shortly after the start of hostilities, Salvadoran citizen Archie Baldocchi was obliged to 'sell' his privately owned North American P-51D to the FAS. Wearing essentially the civil paint scheme that the owner had applied, it was equipped with armament and used in operations as FAS-402, the second use of this serial. (Archie Baldocchi)

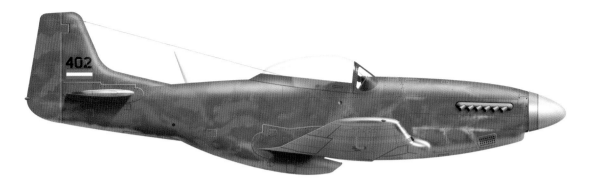

North American P-51D Mustang, coded 'FAS-402', Fuerza Aérea Salvadoreña, El Salvador, early 1970s

ABOVE /BELOW: The former civil P-51D, FAS-402, after the end of hostilities in two variations of warpaint. (Archie Baldocchi top and Guido E. Buehlmann below)

Also from Hikoki Publications

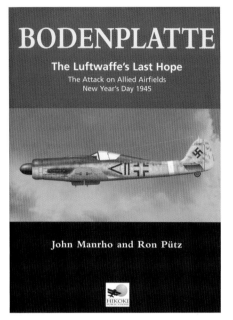

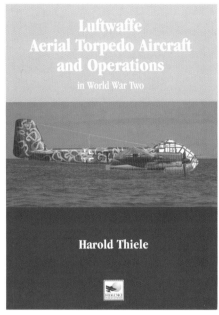

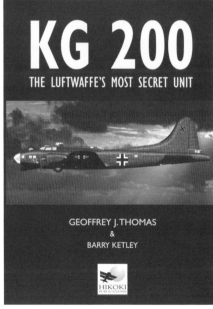

www.hikokiwarplanes.com